Children and Youth in the Catechumenate

Forming Young Disciples for Mission

Anne Y. Koester

LITURGICAL PRESS
Collegeville, Minnesota

www.litpress.org

1 2 3 4 5 6 7 8 9

Library of Congress Cataloging-in-Publication Data

Names: Koester, Anne Y., author.
Title: Children and youth in the catechumenate : forming young disciples for mission / Anne Y. Koester.
Description: Collegeville, Minnesota : Liturgical Press, [2021] | Summary: "By using the liturgy of the church and the liturgy of life, Anne Koester demonstrates the four integral dimensions of Christian discipleship that form young believers for mission" — Provided by publisher.
Identifiers: LCCN 2021014613 (print) | LCCN 2021014614 (ebook) | ISBN 9780814666227 (paperback) | ISBN 9780814666487 (epub) | ISBN 9780814666487 (mobi) | ISBN 9780814666487 (pdf)
Subjects: LCSH: Christian education of children. | Initiation rites—Religious aspects—Catholic Church. | Catholic Church—Liturgy. | Catechumens—Religious life. | Children—Religious life. | Youth—Religious life.
Classification: LCC BX926.3 .K64 2021 (print) | LCC BX926.3 (ebook) | DDC 268/.432—dc23
LC record available at https://lccn.loc.gov/2021014613
LC ebook record available at https://lccn.loc.gov/2021014614

"The challenging task of evangelization is one that belongs to every baptized member of the Body of Christ. In order to be sensitive to the needs of every generation, an evangelizing church must continually assess and renew the way it forms disciples. Anne Koester's exploration of the Rite of Christian Initiation of Adults as adapted for young children and teens does just that. Koester demonstrates with great expertise and ministerial backbone how the work of initiation is a process of apprenticeship, helping young people to experience real conversion by practicing the Christian life and assisting the already baptized in their role as companions on the journey. This resource is a must-read for pastors and religious educators who struggle with how to best incorporate young people into the one catechumenate of the local parish."

—Stephen S. Wilbricht, CSC, Associate Professor of Theology, Stonehill College

"Anne Koester has filled a vital need in the literature on the initiation of children of catechumenal age. She rightly insists that their formation must be catechetical, liturgical, communal, and apostolic; that we must take their conversion seriously; and that we focus on their experience of engaging the faith in action. All ministers of initiation will be well served in this straightforward review of the RCIA process for this age group."

—Catherine Vincie, RSHM, PhD

"A must-read for those involved in implementing the catechumenate adapted for children and youth. Attention to critical pastoral questions inspires a return to the ritual text for Christian initiation that informs pastoral decisions about authentic adaptation that leads to discipleship. It will be required reading in my course on the catechumenate for pastoral ministers."

—Diana Dudoit Raiche, University of Dallas

"Among Catholics, the presence of unbaptized children and youth used to be a rarity. Now any parish may encounter a member of this group any day. Not every parish is ready. Anne Koester's book shares her experience ministering to young inquirers and their families. It teems with accurate knowledge of the RCIA, a vision of intergenerational parish life, a catechist's ability to inform and inspire, and an uncanny sense of what your next question will be. Even if you are familiar with the RCIA adapted for children, this book will guide you to fuller ministry."

—Father Paul Turner, Pastor
Cathedral of the Immaculate Conception, Kansas City, Missouri
Author of *When Other Christians Become Catholic*

"This book offers solid insights into the process of Christian initiation for adults and children, accompanied by a wealth of practical questions and suggestions to help parish RCIA teams guide children and teens on the path to conversion and faith. Anyone working with young people seeking to join the Catholic Church and celebrate the sacraments of initiation will find this book quite helpful."

—Fr. Lawrence E. Mick, author *RCIA: How Are We Doing?*,
is a priest of the Archdiocese of Cincinnati

Contents

Acknowledgments vii

PART ONE

Chapter 1
Critical Questions 1

Chapter 2
Starting Points 7

Chapter 3
Roles and Responsibilities 15

Chapter 4
Faith and Conversion 32

PART TWO

Chapter 5
Period of Evangelization and Precatechumenate 41

Chapter 6
First Ritual Step: Acceptance into the Order of Catechumens 59

PART THREE

Chapter 7
Period of the Catechumenate 65

Chapter 8
Second Ritual Step: Election or Enrollment of Names 81

PART FOUR

Chapter 9
Period of Purification and Enlightenment 85

Chapter 10
Third Ritual Step: Celebration of the Sacraments of Initiation 92

PART FIVE

Chapter 11
Period of Postbaptismal Catechesis or Mystagogy 97

Acknowledgments

With Much Gratitude

. . . to my sister, Sue Koester, for her encouragement and toleration;

. . . to my friend, Mary Schaffer, for reading drafts and providing thoughtful comments;

. . . to the many passionate and faithful parish catechists and leaders who journey with those seeking Christian initiation in the Catholic Church.

PART ONE

Chapter 1

Critical Questions

I can still remember the weekend in the fall of 1988 when I was recruited to make a post-Communion announcement during Mass about the newly mandated *Rite of Christian Initiation of Adults* (RCIA). Although I was new on the catechumenate team, the RCIA process had been in place for several years at the parish; some parishioners might have wondered what the big deal was.

At the same time, however, I distinctly remember noting that the catechumenate was also available to children "of catechetical age, around age seven." I announced it as though it were something new, not realizing that the 1972 *Ordo* included a section on the initiation of children of catechetical age who were not baptized. I recall that the conversations among parish staff about the implementation strategy for the catechumenate adapted for children[1] quickly gained momentum. Although the parish liturgy director

1. The formal title for part II, chapter 1 of the RCIA is "Christian Initiation of Children Who Have Reached Catechetical Age." It is commonly known as the "RCIA adapted for children."

had oversight responsibilities for the RCIA—as a liturgical order of the church—responsibilities for the RCIA process adapted for children fell to the director of religious education.

At the time, the parish had to feel its way with what to do about the faith formation of the children seeking baptism, as well as those who were already baptized and seeking full communion with the Catholic Church. Would their formation be with the children in the religious education program? Would we include the "RCIA children" in the rituals celebrated with the adults? Admittedly, it involved some trial and error, as it no doubt did for many parishes. As I think about the children who participated in the process in the 1980s, it is sobering to realize that they would be in their forties now. I pray that they are committed and active Christian disciples who are engaged in the life of the church and its mission.

A generation later, where are we with the catechumenate adapted for children? While much has been learned in the decades since parishes began to implement the RCIA process adapted for children, we need to continue to probe the depths of the rite, reflect on its vision, educate and involve our parish communities, and imagine anew effective ways of forming children and youth as Christian disciples. The continuous nature of this work respects the fact that conversion is a dynamic and unpredictable process and that we live in an ever-changing world that presents both challenges and opportunities for people of faith from all generations.

I suggest that we keep before us what I see as several enduring and critical questions about our implementation of the catechumenate adapted for children:

- First, what does *Christian conversion* look like for children and youth? The catechumenate, after all, is a conversion process, which may strike us as a very adult experience. And yet, the RCIA process adapted for children is likewise at its core a conversion process. How do we speak about conversion for children and youth, and how do we help them name experiences of conversion? Further, how do we impress upon them that in the Catholic imagination conversion is a way of life?

- Conversion assumes active discernment, a prayerful sorting out of the movements of the Spirit. What does discernment mean for a child or teen, and how do we support them in their discernment about initiation into the Christian way of life?
- How best do we help children and youth pray and foster a desire to be people of prayer as they grow? In what ways can we help them imagine their lives as prayer?
- Catholics see liturgy as the source and summit of church life. How do we instill in children and youth a love for the church's liturgy and an awareness of the liturgy of life? How might our celebrations of the catechumenate rituals and sacraments of initiation form lifelong active participants in the church's liturgy and in the liturgy of life?
- The community is central to Catholic identity. How do we impress upon children and youth the value of the community and encourage their ongoing engagement with parish life? Can we assist them with identifying their gifts and ways in which these gifts can be placed at the service of the parish community right now, regardless of their age? Early involvement in the parish community and its outreach to the local community and beyond might just mean future involvement as adults, not to mention, leaders.
- How do we prepare children and youth to live the Christian life in the Catholic tradition? What do we ourselves understand about what this means, and how do we lead children and youth to grasp the contours of the Catholic Christian life?
- As baptized persons, we are constantly *becoming* Christian disciples. Discipleship is something we never fully master; however, if we are truly committed to living out of our baptism, we are experienced enough to take on apprentices. The RCIA process is teeming with apprentices—adults at various stages in life and, yes, children and youth. In fact, it's what they sign up for—to begin and gradually embrace the process of becoming Christian disciples. Look at the very clear and

compelling description of the catechumenate in the Catholic Church's Decree on the Mission Activity of the Church (*Ad Gentes*): "The catechumenate . . . is not merely an exposition of dogmatic truths and norms of morality, but a period of formation in the entire christian life, an apprenticeship of suitable duration, during which the disciples will be joined to Christ their teacher" (14). Do we see the children and youth we work with as apprentices in the Christian life? How do we go about preparing them for the work of discipleship? What does this overall conviction mean for our approach to faith formation and catechesis? How do we root faith formation and catechesis in liturgy and in mission?

- What is the purpose of the rituals that punctuate the conversion process? Are these rituals celebrated with full and meaningful symbols and with the presence of the community? Do the rituals serve to deepen and express the experience of conversion and at the same time form the young disciples-in-training to further the church's mission in the world? In other words, are the rituals understood as an essential source of learning and formation in the school of discipleship?
- We will find a significant cast of participants in the catechumenate adapted for children. There are parents, guardians and extended families, godparents or sponsors, peer companions and the parish community. What are the roles of these various groups of people in the apprenticeship for the children and youth seeking Christian initiation?

Whew! That's a lot of questions! How do we get to what the rite envisions? First, we must keep in mind that this is God's work. We are along for the ride, trying to give the process of conversion and the making of disciples a little structure, and supporting the young apprentices on their journey of faith.

Second, we need a framework for the process of conversion and for the apprenticeship that will characterize it. We will want to turn first to RCIA 75, which provides an approach that is:

- catechetical
- communal
- liturgical
- and apostolic

In other words, it is an approach that immerses the catechumens/apprentices in the life of the community, the liturgy of the church, and the liturgy of life. These dimensions should be approached as a whole; we cannot isolate one from the other. It's one piece. Each dimension shapes and informs the others and each is integral to the experience of ongoing conversion and faith development.

Other texts of the Catholic Church, including *Ad Gentes* and the *Directory for Catechesis*, support this four-pronged approach. We need to sit with the *Rite of Christian Initiation of Adults* and these other texts. And then sit with them again—*and* again. We need to read and reread them, share and discuss them with our catechists, pastoral staff, and parish at large.

Everyone is enrolled in this school of discipleship, and everyone needs to be committed to an approach to the catechumenate adapted for children that is grounded in the church's liturgy and apostolic mission. Our desire should be to contribute to the formation of these young apprentices' identity as the Body of Christ, the church—an identity that will order all aspects of their lives. We are forming them for mission, to live as "other Christs"[2] in the world.

In this volume, we will explore the RCIA process adapted for children, including: its history, albeit briefly; who the young apprentices are that the rite envisions and who, in fact, they are in our parishes; the roles of parents, guardians, families, godparents and sponsors, and the community, including the peers of the children and youth; how we might speak about conversion and coming

2. I am borrowing this phrase from Virgil Michel, OSB, pioneer of the modern liturgical movement in the United States, in his "Liturgy and the Catholic Life," unpublished MS, 78 and 136.

to faith; and a holistic approach to the process that is "aimed at training them in the Christian life" (RCIA 75).

My primary focus will be on children and youth who are seeking initiation into the Body of Christ. As we know from experience, these are not the only young apprentices who participate in the RCIA process adapted for children. There are also those who were baptized in the Catholic Church but who have received little or no formal faith formation and who have not participated in sacramental rituals beyond baptism. In addition, there are children and youth who were baptized in another ecclesial community and who are seeking to be received into the full communion of the Catholic Church. While not the focus of this book, these groups of young apprentices will be discussed at times, because of the overlap—and sometimes confusion—with the apprentices in the catechumenate.

Chapter 2

Starting Points

A Splash of History

In response to the Second Vatican Council's mandate to restore the catechumenate for adults, the Roman Catholic Church promulgated the first Latin edition of the *Ordo Initiationis Christianae Adultorum* in 1972. The text was published in English in 1974 as the *Rite of Christian Initiation of Adults;* this translation was provisional but was used as the approved rite for more than ten years. The 1972 *Ordo* and its English translation included a section on the initiation of unbaptized children of catechetical age. At the time, the inclusion of children of catechetical age barely registered with pastoral leaders. The focus was on adults seeking Christian initiation as this new order was gradually introduced to parishes in the United States from the mid-1970s to the mid-1980s.

In 1986, the US bishops approved additions to the RCIA, including rites for the already baptized seeking full communion with the Catholic Church, along with the National Statutes for the Catechumenate and a plan for implementation of the RCIA. In 1988, the final English translation was approved and mandated for all parishes. It is important to note that at the time of the writing of this book, the 1972 *Ordo* is in the process of being retranslated. Since the final retranslated text is not yet available, the references to the RCIA here are to the 1988 United States of America translation.

As mentioned, the drafters of the 1972 *Ordo* included a section on the initiation of unbaptized children of catechetical age. Thomas Morris tells us that this was a "rushed addition to the ritual text," and, in fact, the drafters did not think this variant would be used much.[1] The haste might explain, at least in part, the anomalies we find in the provisions of the rite that are specific to children, such as a penitential rite, rather than the Rite of Election, named as the second ritual step and as a "kind of scrutiny." We will return to these incongruities later.

In the late 1960s, when the *Ordo* was drafted, those who worked on the rite likely could not have imagined the extent to which the rite has been and is adapted for children in the church decades later. What was intended to be a little-used variant has been fully integrated into parish life in many places, just as the process for adults has. One also has the impression, when studying the section on the Christian initiation of children who have reached catechetical age, that the drafters had in mind children who are around what is typically considered to be "First Communion age," that is, around seven or eight years old. Notably, at the time the rite was drafted, children in many European countries were baptized as infants and then confirmed and shared in the Eucharist for the first time at the age of seven or eight. Paul Turner points out that the working group "envisioned that unbaptized children of catechetical age would be preparing for confirmation and First Communion at the same time as their Catholic peers"; they did not anticipate that the age of confirmation would rise well beyond catechetical age,[2] as we see in the majority of US dioceses today.

1. Thomas H. Morris, "Christian Initiation of Children: Some Pastoral Questions," *Catechumenate* 19 (1997): 17.

2. Paul Turner, "MyRCIA: The Meaning of Adult Initiation in Post–Vatican II America," https://paulturner.org/wp-content/uploads/2014/10/MyRCIA-web-site.pdf.

In reality, the age of children and youth seeking Christian initiation runs the gamut. I marvel at this every year when I see the number and various ages of children and teens at the Rite of Election in the Archdiocese of Washington. To witness these children and teens come forward and take their place alongside adults preparing for initiation is truly inspiring. We can speculate on the factors that play into both the number and wide range of ages of children and youth who seek Christian initiation today. For instance, even if one is or both are Catholic, some parents choose to wait to have their children baptized; they sometimes reason that they want their children to choose their religious affiliation for themselves. While this reasoning does not square with Catholic theology of the baptism of children, it nevertheless reflects current cultural influences.

Baptism might also be delayed when parents in ecumenical or interreligious marriages have not yet come to an agreement on the religious upbringing of their children. It is also possible that the family lived in a place or in circumstances that made it unsafe for them to openly practice their faith.

And finally, let's face it: some Catholic parents are in their own struggle with the Catholic Church, unsure of whether they themselves can remain active participants. This, too, may lead some to postpone the initiation of their children. We need to be aware of these circumstances so we are prepared for sometimes complex and sensitive conversations with parents when they arrive on our doorsteps with their young children or teenagers who are asking for baptism. We will circle back to this when we talk about the role of parents in the catechumenate adapted for children.

Who Are the Children (and Youth)?

Part II, chapter 1 (252–330) of the 1988 rite is titled "Christian Initiation of Children Who Have Reached Catechetical Age." Who are these children? We look first to paragraph 252:

> This form of the rite of Christian initiation is intended for children, not baptized as infants, *who have attained the use of reason*

> *and are of catechetical age.* They seek Christian initiation either at the direction of their parents or guardians or, *with* parental permission, on their own initiative. *Such children are capable of receiving and nurturing a personal faith and of recognizing an obligation in conscience.* But they cannot yet be treated as adults because, at this stage of their lives, they are dependent on their parents or guardians and are still strongly influenced by their companions and their social surroundings. (Emphases mine.)

Initially, we need to address the questions of at what age does a child "attain the use of reason" and when are they considered to be "of catechetical age"? In short, it's not clear. Are these simultaneous realities? Not always. Let's take a closer look.

The rite itself does not define "use of reason," and it added a new term, "catechetical age," to the criteria. How are we to understand these terms in pinpointing when a child is eligible for the rite adapted for children? Paul Turner points out that historically, "'use of reason' was used to describe the age at which one could distinguish ordinary from spiritual food, and hence was ready to share communion." However, he also notes that a mistake was made in the English translation of RCIA 252. The Latin words *aetatem discretionis* were translated not as "age of discretion" but as "use of reason." "Age of discretion" has been associated with the ability to distinguish right from wrong and readiness for the sacraments of reconciliation and confirmation (since confession is encouraged before one is confirmed). Turner argues that "catechetical age" as used in the rite is equated with "age of discretion." "At that age," he adds, "one could prepare for the initiation rites; and one would logically celebrate them by the age of the use of reason."[3]

There are a few more pieces to this puzzle. Canons 11 and 97 §2 of the *Code of Canon Law* set the age of the use of reason at age seven.[4] Yet, canonist Ladislas Orsy notes that there is not a precise

3. Turner, "Envy and the Confirmation of Children of Catechetical Age," https://paulturner.org/wp-content/uploads/2012/08/envy_confirmation.htm.

4. For example, canon 97 §2 states that "with the completion of the seventh year one is presumed to have the use of reason."

moment that we can identify for when a child receives the use of reason; he adds that "if this is so, the age of seven is arbitrary."[5] So while there is a presumption of the "use of reason" with the completion of the seventh year, it is possible that a child younger than seven can have the use of reason and that the child's formation should then follow the general pattern of the catechumenate, with the appropriate adaptations made (see the 1986 National Conference of Catholic Bishops' National Statutes, 18).

It is also important to be familiar with the US bishops' *Guidelines for the Celebration of the Sacraments with Persons with Disabilities*. Paragraph 13 of the *Guidelines* provides:

> "The Initiation of catechumens is a gradual process that takes place within the community of the faithful." Adults and children of catechetical age with disabilities should be welcomed into all stages and rites of the initiation process. If the catechumen is of catechetical age, the rites may be adapted according to need. In these cases, catechesis for persons with disabilities must be adapted in content and method to their particular situations. Like others, adults and children of catechetical age with disabilities should normally receive the Sacraments of Baptism, Confirmation, and Eucharist in a single celebration.[6]

The phrase "use of reason" does not appear in this paragraph providing guidance on the Christian initiation of children of catechetical age with differing abilities; however, canon 852 §1 of the *Code of Canon Law*, which does reference "use of reason," is cited in the footnotes: "What is prescribed in the canons on the baptism of an adult is applicable to all who are no longer infants but have attained the use of reason."[7] Finally—and importantly—paragraph 13

5. Ladislas Orsy, "Title I: Ecclesiastical Laws (cc. 7–22)," in *The Code of Canon Law: A Text and Commentary*, ed. James A. Coriden, Thomas J. Green, and Donald E. Heintschel, 72 (New York: Paulist Press, 1985).

6. *Guidelines for the Celebration of the Sacraments with Persons with Disabilities* (June 15, 2017), 13, quoting RCIA 4.

7. See *Guidelines*, n. 18.

of the *Guidelines* specifies that children of catechetical age with disabilities should normally be fully initiated through the sacraments of baptism, confirmation, and Eucharist in a single celebration.

Returning to the language of RCIA 252, we also see that it presumed that children who have attained the use of reason and are of catechetical age and who seek Christian initiation at the direction of their parents or, with parental consent, on their own, are thought to be "capable of receiving and nurturing a personal faith and of recognizing an obligation in conscience," meaning they are presumed to be able to grow in personal faith and are capable of conversion. We will consider in more detail later on the experiences of faith and conversion.

So where does this leave us? Generally speaking, the minimum age for children to participate in the catechumenate process adapted for children is around the seventh year, but we should remember that a child younger than seven can attain the use of reason and be of catechetical age, just as a child older than age seven might not yet be ready to prepare for Christian initiation. This will require conversation with the child and parents or guardians and the willingness to "make full and wise use of the options mentioned in *Christian Initiation*, General Introduction (nos. 34–35)."[8]

I think what is also important here in discerning readiness of a child at this lower end of the age spectrum for minors is that we resist tying their readiness for the sacraments of initiation to their year in school simply so they can be with their Catholic classmates for religious education classes and participate in rituals at or about the same time, be it First Communion or confirmation. We owe it

8. RCIA 259. *Christian Initiation*, General Introduction 34 provides: "Taking into account existing circumstances and other needs, as well as the wishes of the faithful, the minister should make full use of the various options allowed in the rite." Paragraph 35 states: "In addition to the adaptations that are provided in the Roman Ritual for the dialogue and blessings, the minister may make other adaptations for special circumstances. These adaptations will be indicated more fully in the Introductions to the rites of baptism for adults and for children."

to these children and youth to meet them where they are and walk the journey of conversion with them at their own pace.

Already Baptized Children and Youth

As mentioned, I will primarily focus on children and youth who are not baptized. There are, of course, other apprentices in the Christian life who participate in the RCIA process. RCIA part II, chapter 4 pertains to individuals who were baptized in the Catholic Church but who have received little or no formal faith formation and who have not participated in sacramental rituals beyond baptism. With respect to children, this section is generally adapted for those who are older than the usual First Communion age and often who meet the minimum age that a particular diocese requires for confirmation. In addition, RCIA part II, chapter 5 concerns persons baptized in another ecclesial community and who are seeking to be received into the full communion of the Catholic Church. "Infants" (generally before the seventh year) baptized in another Christian community are received into full communion without a rite, but simply at the request of their parents or guardians. However, children of "catechetical age" participate in the RCIA adapted for children and are received into full communion just as baptized adults are—through a profession of faith and act of reception, which is then followed immediately by the sacraments of confirmation and Eucharist.

The Relationship between RCIA Part I and Part II, Chapter 1

It needs to be underscored that the RCIA process adapted for children is not a separate order. Note the opening words of RCIA 252, which begin part II, chapter 1 with "This form of the rite . . ." This section is an adaptation of the primary text, part I (RCIA 1–251). Therefore, we cannot turn to the paragraphs focused on the initiation of children (RCIA 252–330) and treat them as independent from part I. Part II, chapter 1 must always be interpreted and implemented in the context of part I. If there is a conflict between the two, we must defer to part I; or if part II is unclear, we must again defer to part I.

As we continue our exploration of children and youth in the catechumenate, we will also want to keep in front of us other significant texts that need to be read in conjunction with the RCIA: *Ad Gentes* (Decree on the Mission Activity of the Church) 1965, the *National Directory for Catechesis* 2005, and the *Directory for Catechesis* 2020. These documents further emphasize an approach to Christian initiation that forms catechumens for the work of discipleship.

Chapter 3

Roles and Responsibilities

It was a family affair. The first to arrive at the doorstep of the parish were Dena and her sons, Jonah, age nine, and Ian, age seven. Dena was baptized in the Methodist Church but had not been actively engaged with a Christian faith community for several years. She was searching for a church home for her family. Dena decided to begin the RCIA process to explore the possibility of being received into the full communion of the Catholic Church. At the same time, Jonah and Ian, who were not baptized, began the catechumenate process adapted for children. A couple of months into the process for Dena and her sons, Dena's fiancé, Jayden, started accompanying them to Sunday Mass. Jayden was raised in the Southern Baptist tradition but was never baptized. He was skeptical of the Catholic Church but supportive of Dena's desire to explore becoming Catholic and of her sons' preparation for the rites of Christian initiation. Jayden preferred to keep a low profile, yet he came to the parish regularly with Dena and the boys. So we're not all left in suspense . . . happily, Jayden started the catechumenate process a year later and was baptized.

Another story—similar but with differences. Jane contacted the parish to say that her fourteen-year-old son, Michael, wanted to be baptized in the Catholic Church. This was at Michael's initiative. Jane reported that he expressed this desire repeatedly for several months, which assured her that he was sincere about it. Jane was baptized in the Baptist tradition; her husband who was Michael's dad was Episcopalian. Michael and his twin sister, Alicia, were exposed to a variety of Christian traditions through their parents and grandparents, but given their parents' different backgrounds, Mom and Dad decided to let Michael and Alicia make their own decisions about baptism when they were ready. Michael was ready. He wanted to explore the Catholic Church because he felt especially close to a Catholic uncle and cousins. Michael's attraction to the Catholic Church and the conversations with his parents even before he and his mom came to the parish led his mom to reflect upon her own faith journey. She did not feel rooted anywhere at the time and was moved by Michael's desire for baptism in the Catholic Church. So, not unlike Dena and her boys, Jane began the RCIA process to seek full communion with the Catholic Church. But unlike the situation with Dena, the "child" here was a teenager, a high school student who was dreaming of becoming an engineer. There's more to this story, too. Michael was a source of evangelization not only for his mom but for his twin sister. The following year, Alicia, age fifteen, participated in the catechumenate and celebrated the rites of initiation. The twins' dad, while fully supportive of their decision to become Catholic, remained active in the Episcopal Church.

One last story. Ben's dad called the parish one day to ask about the path for his nearly seventeen-year-old son to become Catholic. Dad himself was Catholic but inactive. He supported Ben's search but did not want to be involved in the process. Ben commuted to the parish on his own to participate in faith formation. The dad came to the parish for the first time on the day Ben was initiated into the church. Clearly, Ben needed the support of a sponsor and the community throughout the process, since his dad preferred to stay in the background.

I tell these stories because they point to some of the complexities that families potentially bring to our parishes when a child or youth seeks baptism. The stories surface questions such as: What is the role of the parent(s)/guardian(s) in the process of initiation? What if one or both parents are themselves seeking to become Catholic? What if they are not? What if they are Catholic but inactive and unwilling to participate directly with their child in the initiation process? When and why does a sponsor and/or godparent enter the picture? What is their role? The RCIA adapted for children also speaks about "companions." Who are they and what are the expectations for these companions? Obviously, these companions will be different for different ages of catechumens. It's one thing to have children in the process who are around First Communion age; it's an entirely different matter when they are teenagers like Michael, Alicia, and Ben.

First Conversations

Before we look in detail at the roles of parents/guardians, sponsors, godparents, and peer companions, let us consider the initial contact and possible first conversations with parents or guardians and the children and/or youth they bring to our parishes for initiation. Of course, the conversations will be as different as the people who come to us. We all know as pastoral ministers that people bring a lot of living to the church, which makes each family's situation unique. To prepare us to listen and respond to their stories and questions, it will be helpful to imagine some of the scenarios they might present to us.

Is There Parental (or Guardian) Permission?

We need to address this question first because it is a prerequisite to children or youth participating in the catechumenate. Permission from parents or guardians is required for a child or youth to seek Christian initiation, even when the child or youth, as was the case with the teenagers in the stories above, takes the initiative in indicating their desire for baptism. Canon 97 §1 defines an individual under the age of eighteen as a minor, and canon 98 §2 states that a minor remains subject to the authority of parents or guardians. The RCIA adds the requirement of a parent's or guardian's permission in the initiation text itself in paragraphs 252 and 254.2.

In the stories presented, parental permission was not an issue. Jonah and Ian sought initiation willingly but at the direction of their mom, Dena. Michael and Alicia took the initiative in seeking Christian initiation but with their parents' permission—and their mom's own participation in the process. Ben's dad contacted the parish first to state his consent but then left it to Ben.

Of course, permission is not necessarily straightforward in every situation. What if someone other than a parent or guardian accompanies the child or youth to the parish to ask about initiation—a grandparent or other relative, for example? We will want to be prepared to ask whether the parents or guardians have given consent and, if so, discuss how that will be made evident during the process. For example, will the parents or guardians be present for the rituals?

It is a potential red flag if the person accompanying the child or youth does not know or has not asked whether there is parental or guardian permission. We will need to counsel them about the requirement for such permission and inquire whether it can be obtained. We might uncover some complex family dynamics here. Yet, for the child or youth to move forward with seeking initiation, a parent or guardian must give permission. A lack of permission (and maybe even the lack of knowledge about what is happening with their child) might create or contribute to disharmony within the family.

What Faith Background(s) Do the Parents or Guardians Bring?

The catechumenate adapted for children presumes the presence of parents or guardians and notes that their child's progress in faith formation depends on the influence of their parents [or guardians] (RCIA 254). Further, it is "hoped that the children will also receive as much help and example as possible from the parents [or guardians]" (RCIA 254.2). Given this, it will be important to learn what the parents or guardians bring to the process. In particular, it will be helpful to talk with them about their own journey of faith. Some possible questions are:

- What is the faith background of each of the parents or guardians? Are they actively engaged with a particular religious tradition or faith community?
- Is one or both parents or guardians Catholic? Have they always been Catholic, or did they come into the Catholic Church through the RCIA process? Are they active in a parish? If they are inactive or feel alienated from the church, are they seeking to return to active participation in the Catholic Church? If so, who in the parish is available to assist them with this process? Is there an avenue for returning Catholics such as the *Landings*[1] program? It will be vital for their pastoral needs to be addressed apart from the catechumenate adapted for children so their issues do not become entangled with their child's faith formation process.
- If one or both parents or guardians are Catholic and wish not to be involved, what is underneath this and will it negatively affect the child's experience? How do they intend to accompany and support their child in living the Christian life in the Catholic tradition if they themselves are struggling with or indifferent to the church? Who in the parish can respond to these pastoral concerns so they don't become ensnared with the child's experience? Whatever the complexities are, the parents or guardians should be welcomed in the spirit of Christian hospitality and given space to work out their relationship with the church. This may be an opportunity for healing and return to active participation in the church.
- If one or both parents or guardians are other than Catholic, do they want to explore the RCIA process themselves? This was certainly the case with Dena and Jane from the opening

1. *Landings* International, https://landingsintl.org/returning-to-the-church/.

stories. They discerned with the catechists that participating in the RCIA process at the same time as their sons were preparing for initiation would be most beneficial for their family.

Further, it set in motion a lot of sharing in the home and a robust engagement in the life of the parish. If a parent or guardian who is other than Catholic is not interested in exploring the Catholic Church, there is no requirement that they be and they can still fulfill their responsibilities in the initiation process, perhaps with the support of a sponsor or godparent, which will be discussed later.

Michael and Alicia's dad is such an example. He was a committed Episcopalian but fully supported his children's decision to become Catholic. When their mom, Jane, could not accompany them to Mass on Sundays, he came with them. And even more importantly, he was a strong Christian model for his children in the life he led. Moreover, Michael and Alicia had godparents who also participated in the process with them.

- What if a parent or guardian is a non-believer or does not value religious affiliation? The critical question here will be how this will impact the child or youth's experience. Assuming permission has been given, will the parent be able to sincerely support their child's participation in the process and in the church once their child is initiated? Are there particular concerns or challenges here that should be discussed to clarify perceptions and presumptions (maybe about the Catholic Church in general) and to ensure that the parent/guardian's perspectives do not interfere with their child's journey of conversion?

What Are Other Family Dynamics That Might Impact the Process for the Child or Youth and Their Living the Christian Life?

The child or youth's network of relationships might be messy. What dynamics within the family or in the child or youth's wider social circle will be important for us to understand? Some possibilities:

- Are the parents or guardians the primary teachers of faith for the child or youth, or are there others who play a significant role, for example, grandparents, siblings, extended family members, teachers, or other mentors? Do they live in the same household as the child or youth? Are they, and not the parents, accompanying the child or youth at the time they come to the parish to ask about initiation? What role will they have in the catechumenate process? Will they participate in the formational activities and in the rituals that punctuate the process? Will they serve as godparents or sponsors?
- It may also be important to learn whether there are strained or broken relationships within the child or youth's immediate family. If, for example, the child or youth's parents are separated or divorced, what will be the impact? It could affect the child or youth's regular participation in the process if they need to spend time with a parent who lives elsewhere or who is not committed to ensuring their child's participation in the initiation process.
- As was the case with two of the families described at the beginning of this chapter, there is sometimes more than one child or youth from same family who seeks initiation. I think we need to be careful not to assume they will experience the process in the same way or will be on the same timeline or trajectory for initiation. I admit that with Jonah and Ian, parish leaders assumed they would be ready for initiation at the same time, especially since their mom was also in the RCIA process. We needed to do better. Discernment must focus on each individual child and youth, as well as each adult family member who are simultaneously participating in the RCIA process.

What Questions Might the Parents or Guardians and the Child or Youth Bring?

We can expect that parents or guardians and the child or youth seeking initiation will come with many questions. What the catechumenate process involves is not necessarily common knowledge—even among active Catholics. We might anticipate questions from the parents or guardians such as:

- **"Why can't my child be baptized right now?"** They may be familiar with the practices of some Christian communions that allow for individuals to be baptized perhaps within a couple of months after expressing their desire. Naturally, they will want to know why in the Catholic Church it may take a year or more. It will be important first to acknowledge that their question is a valid one. We will then want to help them understand the meaning and purpose of the catechumenate and be prepared to talk about the Catholic Church's perspectives on conversion and faith formation as a process, the role of the community in this process, and the need for rituals along the way to help their child or youth—and the family—name what is happening to them.
- **"Can my child be initiated at the same time their Catholic classmates or friends at the parish receive First Communion or are confirmed?"** Some parents or guardians might even insist upon it. How do we dissuade them from this thinking and yet reassure them of the importance of their child's peers to the process of preparation for initiation and of focusing on their child's needs, which are different from their baptized classmates and friends? Their child's formational needs and readiness for initiation must be the primary consideration.
- **"All of my children want to become Catholic. Will they be baptized at the same time?"** As already mentioned, we need to be careful not to assume that children from the same family will experience the process in the same way or will be on the same timeline or trajectory for initiation. That said, we should also be open to working through whatever concerns a family may have if one child is initiated at the next Easter Vigil and the other one, two, or more are not ready. Will this create logistical issues for the family? What other possible burdens do they foresee? This is not to say we promise that

all of the children will be initiated at the same time, because it remains important to discern readiness with each child. However, it is critical to talk about this at the beginning of the process and not surprise the family with a first-time conversation about it on the threshold of Lent.

- **"Will we need to come with our child to Sunday Mass and whatever else will be involved with preparing for baptism? What if we are not Catholic? Can my child's Catholic grandparent come instead?"** These questions are critical and lead us to examine the role of the parents or guardians as intended in the rite.

The children and teens might have other questions, which we need to hear and discuss with them. For instance, teens might wonder whether they will be with young children in the process. Can they participate in the catechumenate sessions with the adults? Yes, possibly. Or, they might wonder why their parents have to be involved. They might ask whether their best friend can sponsor them. Yes, possibly.

Expectations and Responsibilities of the Parents or Guardians—*and* of Sponsors and Godparents

As a general principle, the Catholic Church sees parents or guardians as the primary teachers of the faith for their children.[2] The RCIA process adapted for children echoes this notion and stresses the role of the parents or guardians, although not always clearly and consistently. Their role and the roles of possible sponsors or godparents seem to overlap at times in the rite and may create some confusion. At the same time, the vagueness of the rite about these roles is perhaps understandable given the complexities, such as those mentioned earlier, that some families bring. Let's take a closer look.

2. See, e.g., chapter 8 of the *Directory for Catechesis* 2020, which highlights the catechetical role of parents.

The rite presumes the presence of parents or guardians in the life of the children and youth seeking initiation. Recall RCIA 252:

> This form of the rite of Christian initiation is intended for children, not baptized as infants, who have attained the use of reason and are of catechetical age. *They seek Christian initiation either at the direction of their parents or guardians or, with parental permission, on their own initiative.* Such children are capable of receiving and nurturing a personal faith and of recognizing an obligation in conscience. *But they cannot yet be treated as adults because, at this stage of their lives, they are dependent on their parents or guardians* and are still strongly influenced by their companions and their social surroundings. (Emphases mine.)

As previously noted, we find in RCIA 254 that the progress of the child or youth in their formation depends on the "influence of their parents,"[3] and:

> *[it] is to be hoped that the children will also receive as much help and example as possible from the parents,* whose permission is required for the children to be initiated and to live the Christian life. The period of initiation will also provide a good opportunity for the family to have contact with priests and catechists. (RCIA 254.2; emphasis mine.)

The rite assumes that the parents or guardians have the primary responsibility for accompanying their child or teen in the process of seeking Christian initiation because, as a minor, the child or youth is dependent on their parents or guardians. The first ministry named for the parents or guardians is to provide their child or teen "as much help and example as possible" (RCIA 254.2).

3. Unfortunately, there is an inconsistency in the rite when it comes to the inclusion of "guardians," as evident in 254.2, which refers only to parents. The same inconsistency occurs in subsequent paragraphs regarding certain rituals (e.g., the Rite of Acceptance into the Order of Catechumens and the Rite of Election). Despite this inconsistency, we should assume that where parents are addressed, guardians are included.

This is the hope. The tentative nature of the language here seems to recognize that some parents or guardians may not be willing to accept the responsibility of walking with their child or teen on the journey of conversion, or perhaps they feel ill-prepared to do so because they themselves are seekers or do not have an active faith life.

When the parents or guardians have given the required permission but are not willing or able to participate in the process with their child or teen, a "sponsor" is identified as the alternative and may act in the place of the parents or guardians. The first time a sponsor is mentioned is in paragraph 260, which introduces the Rite of Acceptance into the Order of Catechumens. RCIA 260 reads, in part:

> When possible, the children's parents or guardians should be present. If they cannot come, they should indicate that they have given consent to their children and their place should be taken by "sponsors" (see no. 10), that is, suitable members of the Church who act on this occasion for the parents and present the children.

RCIA part I, paragraph 10 describes sponsors as "persons who have known and assisted the candidates and stand as witnesses to the candidates' moral character, faith, and intention." These persons might include, for instance, a Catholic grandparent, other relative, or mentor in the child or teen's life. In the absence of such an individual, it might be necessary to ask a parishioner to accompany the child or youth in the catechumenate process.

To illustrate, let's go back to the opening stories. In the case of Jonah and Ian, their mom was present and participated in the process, but as a candidate for reception. Therefore, sponsors from the parish also accompanied the boys in the process. Michael looked to his Catholic uncle to sponsor him, even though his mom, a Baptist becoming Catholic, was also an active participant in the process with Michael. Finally, for Ben, whose dad did not want to participate because he thought of himself as a "lapsed Catholic," a parish sponsor happily accompanied the teen.

Although the rite appears to imply that a sponsor is needed only when a parent or guardian cannot be present—beginning with the Rite of Acceptance into the Order of Catechumens—there is nothing that prohibits a child or youth from having a sponsor even when the parents or guardians are willing to participate in the process. In fact, depending on the circumstances, it might be desirable for the child or youth to have a sponsor as another conversation partner and source of support. This would benefit the parents or guardians, too, especially if they have had little faith formation themselves or have been relatively inactive in a faith community.

Another role is introduced at the time the child or teen is ready to participate in the Rite of Election—that of godparent.[4] Unlike a sponsor in the rite adapted for children, the godparent is not presented as an alternative to the parents or guardians but rather as someone who is present alongside the parents or guardians (or sponsors, if the parents or guardians are not participants).

The General Introduction to *Christian Initiation* describes the role of godparents in the catechumenate for adults as helping them to "persevere in the faith and in their lives as Christians" and in the baptism of children as representing "both the expanded spiritual family of the one to be baptized and the role of the Church as a mother. As occasion offers, godparents help the parents so that children will come to profess the faith and live up to it."[5] For the catechumenate adapted for children, both of these descriptions seem fitting, especially since the age of the catechumens may vary. For youth, for example, godparents can help them, as they would adults, persevere in and live the Christian life. For children, godparents may also be of help to the parents as their young children grow in faith. These responsibilities presume that the godparents

4. RCIA 10 notes the possibility that "it is not the sponsor for the rite of acceptance and the period of the catechumenate but another person who serves as godparent for the periods of purification and enlightenment and of mystagogy." See *Christian Initiation*, General Introduction, 8–10, about the role and qualifications of godparents.

5. *Christian Initiation*, General Introduction, 8.

are individuals who take seriously their own baptism and are models of Christian discipleship. Ideally, the godparents engage regularly in personal prayer and the church's liturgy, attend to their own spiritual growth, and are active participants in the life of the parish and broader community.

During the Rite of Election, the godparents, along with the parents or guardians (or sponsors), testify to the readiness of the children or youth to advance toward the sacraments of initiation (RCIA 278). Godparents are also assumed to be present for the "second step" as it is labeled in the RCIA adapted for children, that of the penitential rites (RCIA 293).[6] The parents or guardians are not mentioned here.

Finally, the godparents are to be present at the rites of initiation. Although the parents or guardians (or sponsors) are all called to the baptismal font with the children or teens (RCIA 310), it is the godparents who touch the children or teens at the moment of baptism (RCIA 317) and present the baptismal garment (RCIA 320) and lighted candle to the newly baptized (RCIA 321). The godparents then stand with the children or teens when they are anointed with chrism (RCIA 326).

Sorting out these adult roles in the rite adapted for children or youth can be a bit tedious. It will be important to discuss the expectations and responsibilities of each early on in the process with the parents or guardians (or other adults who accompany the children or youth) so they and the children or youth can discern who will be involved and what their respective responsibilities will be. To briefly recap:

- What will be the responsibilities of the *parents or guardians*? Will they accompany their children during faith formation sessions? Will they participate in parish or community activities with their children? Will they be present at and participate in the liturgical rituals that are part of the catecheumenate

6. Concerns related to this "second step" of penitential rites are discussed in part four, chapter 9, "Period of Purification and Enlightenment."

process? How will they support their children's conversion process at home? For example, are they prepared to have conversations with their children about matters of faith, pray with them, help them prepare for and reflect upon their experiences of the liturgical rites, and support their children's involvement with outreach activities?

- Is a *sponsor* needed? Recall that the rite provides for a sponsor as an alternative to the parents or guardians when they are unwilling or unable to participate. If a sponsor stands in the place of the parents or guardians, can they fulfill the responsibilities mentioned above? Even when the parents or guardians are actively involved, would a sponsor be beneficial to the child or youth and to the parents or guardians? How might they share in the responsibilities of the parents or guardians?
- The rite also presumes the presence of *godparents* (or godparent, as a catechumen may have *either* a godmother or godfather). From a practical standpoint, a godparent might be the same person as the sponsor. Or the godparent(s) might be other individuals who can testify to the readiness of the children or youth for Christian initiation and help them live as Christian disciples. How will the godparents be involved with the conversion process from the beginning? Will they participate in activities aimed at forming the children or youth as Christian apprentices? How will they be prepared to accompany the children or youth during the rituals, whether all or some of them? What do the children or youth expect of them, and what do the parents or guardians expect of them? These same questions might also be asked about a sponsor.

Expectations and Responsibilities of the Children or Youth's "Companions"

We turn now to the special significance that the text assigns to the "companions" of the children and youth in the catechumenate.

The rite notes that the children or youth are "still strongly influenced by their companions and their social surroundings" (RCIA 252). In fact, the rite stresses that the progress of the young catechumens is dependent not only on the influence of their parents or guardians but also "on the help and example of their companions" (RCIA 254). Who are these companions? What is their role in the catechumenal process?

As mentioned earlier, the section of the rite on the Christian initiation of children leaves one with the impression that the architects of the rite had in mind children who are around "First Communion age" and that they would have baptized Catholic peers who were also preparing for sacramental rites. This is reflected in RCIA 254.1, where the text reads that the children to be initiated "often belong to a group of children of the same age who are already baptized and are preparing for confirmation and eucharist" and that their preparation for initiation "progresses gradually and within the supportive setting of this group of companions."

This presumed group of companions is identified later in the rite as the catechumens' "catechetical group." The "catechetical group" is imagined to be present for the rites of the catechumenal process as representatives of the parish community (see RCIA 257 and 269) and participate in the celebration of penitential rites (RCIA 293). In addition, the text suggests that "if possible," the catechumens "come to the sacraments of initiation at the time that their baptized companions are to receive confirmation or eucharist" (RCIA 256 and 308).[7]

These presumptions about who the companions of the young catechumens are and what their presence and role in the catechumenal process entail surface a host of concerns. For instance, merging the children who are preparing for Christian initiation with baptized peers who are preparing for First Communion or confirmation may confuse and potentially overshadow the catechumenal process. The parish community might not come to know

7. Initiating catechumens at the same time as baptized children or youth celebrate confirmation or Eucharist raises its own issues, which will be addressed later.

the young catechumens, potentially neglecting the community's role of welcoming and supporting them in the process. In addition, the status of the companions as already baptized members of the church might be downplayed.

Moreover, because the number of catechumens is likely to be far fewer than the Catholic children preparing for sacramental celebrations, the program in place to prepare the latter group could easily control the catechetical agenda, when the formational needs of the catechumens are not identical to those who are already baptized.

Combining the young catechumens with this particular peer group might also compromise the discernment called for in the catechumenate process. The catechumens could easily feel pressured to stay with their "catechetical group" and not feel they can speak honestly about their readiness for the sacraments of initiation. Finally, a combined group pushes against a year-round RCIA process with ongoing inquiry. The children and youth who seek Christian initiation would likely be told to wait for the new school or religious education "year" to begin their journey of conversion.

We will say more about a year-round process with ongoing inquiry later; for now, it is enough to say that merging young catechumens with their baptized peers who are preparing for sacramental rituals hampers a parish's ability to immediately welcome those who desire baptism. These children or youth and their families have responded to the movement of the Holy Spirit in their lives; neither they nor the Holy Spirit should have to wait on us.

Naming these concerns is not to say that there is no role for peer companions in the catechumenal process or that their presence would not be mutually beneficial. First, the young catechumens need Christian models. They are indeed influenced by their peers, so the stories, attitudes, behaviors, and ways of speaking of their Catholic companions carry great weight.

Moreover, the baptized peers are enriched by their involvement with the catechumens; they can come to appreciate more deeply their own baptism and their responsibilities for sharing their faith with and accompanying those who are seeking to live the Christian life. Perhaps it is most beneficial to think of these Catholic peers as fellow apprentices and not simply as children or teens in a catechetical group that is preparing for sacramental rites. As fellow apprentices, they might accompany the young catechumens at liturgy and in prayer, invite them to participate in parish activities, and learn alongside them as they discover ways to serve others and together reflect on these experiences. Such accompaniment could certainly extend beyond the catechumenal process to the neophyte year of the newly baptized, establishing a foundation for ongoing friendships and faith sharing.

Chapter 4

Faith and Conversion

Christian initiation is an awakening of faith, a journey of conversion, an unfolding of relationships. So too is the entirety of the Christian life. In other words, these experiences are not isolated and passing moments; they are not accomplishments on the other side of the process of initiation into the Christian community that can be checked off as "completed." Faith and conversion are multifaceted and tightly interwoven experiences that are at once discernable and mysterious. What can we say about these human experiences in general and in particular, and how is faith and conversion experienced in the life of a child or teen? How do we help them tell the stories about their experiences of the mysterious workings of the Holy Spirit? How do we introduce them to the faith of the church and to the reality of conversion as a way of life for Christians? None of this is prescribed or preprogrammed, although the ritual text does give us some clues about the church's understanding of faith and conversion. We will look at these clues in a broader discussion about faith and conversion.

Faith

What comes to mind when you are asked to describe *faith*? A set of concepts about what Christians believe? Something we are to memorize, or something to be *lived*? Is faith acquired through instruction, or is it a gift that is planted in the depths of every human heart, even if unexpressed? And *whose* faith are we talking about? We can speak about the faith of the individual, of course, but what about the faith of Christ and of his church? How do we keep all these dimensions of faith before us?

I turn here to the timeless insights of theologian Mark Searle to help us explore the general contours of *faith*. For Searle, faith is fundamental to the human person. In fact, he contends that it is "already present and shaping our lives before we are conscious of it." Awareness of this foundational faith often comes when there is an experience of crisis, a loss of meaning, when what is "normal" breaks down. Such experiences cause us to realize there is something we cannot quite explain that lies underneath what we think, say, and do, and how we act and react in our world. This basic level of faith is a prereflexive way of living life even before we become aware of it.[1]

Searle further emphasizes that the process of becoming conscious of faith happens at God's initiative, not ours. He writes, "God is doing something for us and in us which we cannot do for ourselves. To come to true faith is to experience the saving presence of God in our lives as pure gift." Faith is our response to this gift, and our response is "as much gift of God as it is our own free commitment."[2] Faith is awakened not through what *we* do but because of what *God* does. Searle explains:

> Faith is not so much a matter of knowledge which can be acquired, but of insight which is given or something which dawns

1. Mark Searle, "Faith and Sacraments in the Conversion Process," in *Conversion and the Catechumenate*, ed. Robert D. Duggan, 66 (Mahwah, NJ: Paulist Press, 1984).

2. Searle, "Faith and Sacraments," 71.

> on a person. The same is true of faith as submission to God. It is not purely the individual's decision alone, but the discovery of being discovered, loved, and called to faith. The very freedom with which we surrender to God is itself God's gift and grace.[3]

What does this mean for catechumens? While it is our responsibility as church to evangelize and invite people to embrace the gift of faith, we cannot "*give* catechumens faith"; rather, we need to "allow their faith to be confronted with the word of God."[4] We might help facilitate this process through our way of accompanying them, keeping in mind that the word of God is proclaimed in multiple ways—for example, through the church's liturgical celebrations, Scripture reflection, faith sharing, parish events, and outreach to people in need.

What is key here is to resist trying to create a syllabus for how catechumens will discover "being discovered, loved, and called to faith." We are to support, not prescribe, the process of discovery. We do this when we invite the catechumens to share their stories and listen to the words and images used, as well as listen to *what lies between* these words and images. Their stories reveal grace. They *teach us* something about God—things we never knew and would not have known except for the unique way in which God has called each catechumen to faith. In their storytelling and in our sharing with them the stories of the church, they come to realize that their stories are part of a larger story of God's faithfulness.

We support the catechumens' process of discovery when they gather with the community for worship. Here, the children and youth further encounter the faith of Christ and the faith of the church. They can discover being loved and called to faith in the midst of a community of people who are on the same journey and who respond to God's invitation through their hospitality, proclamation of God's word, acts of praise and thanksgiving,

3. Mark Searle, *Christening: The Making of Christians* (Collegeville, MN: Liturgical Press, 1980), 48.

4. Searle, "Faith and Sacraments," 67 (emphasis mine).

sharing in the sacramental signs, and being sent to be word and sacrament in the world.

The catechumens' discovery of "being discovered, loved, and called to faith" is supported when we invite their participation in the rites that punctuate the catechumenal journey. Not only is their actual participation essential but so too is what we do to prepare them for these rituals and what we do to help them reflect upon these experiences. These rituals help them to absorb and rehearse a new identity with an assembly that is continually being shaped into this same identity—that is, the Body of Christ. The rituals help them to try on this emerging faith in Christ; as Mark Searle wrote, "Faith in Christ can really be grasped only from the inside, by trying it on."[5]

When we involve these young apprentices in the work of Christian discipleship—whether calling homebound parishioners, delivering groceries to neighbors with food insecurity, taking care of a local park, or assembling school backpacks for children who would otherwise go without—we support their process of discovery. Through such activities and guided reflection upon these activities, they come to recognize Christ in all people, in creation, and in themselves.

Finally, Mark Searle points out that the faith of an individual is not solely about their own relationship with God; rather, "[in] being called to faith by God, one enters into a pattern of life which is already in place. It is in place in the community of believers, the Church, where the journey into God is a way of life." He goes on to say that the faith of the church is not simply about doctrine; faith is expressed through the celebration of word and sacrament, the gathering of the baptized, the care of those who are suffering, the work for justice, and so much more. "It is into that faith-life-toward-God that the catechumen is to be initiated." Searle adds that any "instruction" given is "not to get the catechumens to believe

5. Mark Searle, "Conversion and Initiation into Faith Growth," in *Christian Initiation Resources Reader*, vol. 1: *Precatechumenate* (New York: William H. Sadlier, 1981), 72.

these things . . . but to open them as doors onto the mystery of life toward God."[6] Key to this, he says, is the faith of Christ, who shares in our vocation to hear God's call and respond. The church celebrates the faith of Christ in its liturgy and manifests it in its mission and teachings. "It is into this faith of Christ as lived by the Church that the catechumen is initiated and eventually baptized."[7]

It is striking that one of the optional responses to the question, "What do you ask of God's Church?" in the Rite of Acceptance into the Order of Catechumens (RCIA 50) is "Faith."[8] Think about that for a moment. We suggest that those seeking Christian initiation ask us, the church, for "faith." Again, faith is not a possession we own and can simply dole out to catechumens at will; rather, the catechumens ask us through our life together as liturgical assembly, as witnesses to the Gospel in the world, and as disciples of Christ to support their own discovery of the "faith-life-toward-God" that is our pattern of life as a Christian community.

In response then to the mystery of Christ proclaimed in and by the church, the catechumens "enter the way of faith and conversion as the Holy Spirit opens their hearts" (RCIA 1). *The way* of faith and conversion is not a static, tidy plan or reservoir of information; rather, entering the way of faith and conversion launches one on a dynamic, unpredictable, and life-giving journey into God.

Conversion

As the first paragraph of the RCIA text suggests, faith and conversion are experiences to be held in a fruitful tension. This is further echoed in RCIA 42, which notes that there must be "evidence of the first faith" and "an initial conversion and intention to change their lives and to enter into a relationship with God in Christ" for

6. Searle, "Faith and Sacraments," 69.

7. Searle, "Faith and Sacraments," 71.

8. Note that a different question—"What do you want to become?"—is asked in the section of the text regarding children (see RCIA 264). The rationale for this difference is not apparent. When children or youth are received into the catechumenate with adult catechumens, the dialogue of RCIA 50 should be used.

those seeking initiation to enter into the Order of Catechumens. For children and youth, the conversion required "is personal and somewhat developed, in proportion to their age" (RCIA 253).

Conversion, like faith, can elude exact definition. What might come most immediately to mind is the movement of an individual from no religious belief to religious belief, or from one religious tradition to another. Or perhaps people think of dramatic experiences, such as the conversion of Saint Paul described in the Acts of the Apostles (9:1-22), or stories of conversion in popular culture, such as the one told in Charles Dickens' *A Christmas Carol*. The change of life seems sudden and immediate. But for most people, conversion is experienced without flashes of light or visits from spirits. As Kathleen Hughes observes:

> [T]he first stirrings of conversion surface in our consciousness as a vague awareness that something is missing or something is wrong or something just does not make sense. It can be a nebulous feeling of dissatisfaction or restlessness, or being bogged down, of being unsettled.[9]

I have certainly heard such sentiments expressed by adults who come to the church wanting to explore the Christian life. But what about children and youth? What experiences might be evidence of "first stirrings of conversion"? Again, as indicated in RCIA 253, conversion must be understood according to the developmental level of each child or youth. Also important to consider are the child or youth's experiences in life. There really is no one-size-fits-all template here. For example, some children or youth might in fact experience crisis moments, leading to a search for meaning and belonging. I think of children and youth who have experienced the trauma of food or home insecurity, abuse or bullying, death of a family member, an unstable family life, their own or another's illness, violence in their community, or moving to a new country or state. Or think of adolescents and the sometimes

9. Kathleen Hughes, "Sacraments: Celebrations of the Journey of Conversion," *Supplement to the Way* 94 (1999): 80–81.

confusing or upsetting life changes they experience in their teen years. For others, the journey of conversion might begin very quietly with only whispers in their hearts.

Whatever is happening in the young catechumen's life, conversion is not a once-in-a-lifetime event but a process with various movements and stages that rarely proceed in any predictable order. Like faith, conversion is a gift, initiated by God—again and again. Our job is to model for these young catechumens the ongoing nature of conversion, to help them name their experiences, to reassure them that what is happening is good, and to encourage them in responding to God's invitation.

Further, in the Christian context, conversion is about saving relationships—with God through Jesus Christ and the Holy Spirit, but also with God incarnate in the Body of Christ, the church. Robert Duggan emphasizes that Jesus Christ is at the center of faith development for a child, so their journey must be "filled with stories of Jesus." He asks whether "the child has come to understand and appropriate a relationship with Jesus as the heart and center of the Christian experience."[10] Duggan also points to the ecclesial nature of conversion; catechumens must be inserted into a community of faith.[11] They don't go it alone. The rite itself asserts that initiation is a "gradual process that takes place within the community of the faithful," who join the catechumens "in reflecting on the value of the paschal mystery and by renewing their own conversion, [they] provide an example that will help the catechumens to obey the Holy Spirit more generously" (RCIA 4).

Moreover, the community's rituals help to externalize—"sacramentalize"—the catechumens' experience of conversion.[12] Rituals strengthen the stirrings of faith and mark their progress (see RCIA 6). The rites name, reassure, and communicate meaning, even if the meaning is not yet fully realized.

10. Robert D. Duggan, "Discerning Conversion in Children," in *Issues in the Christian Initiation of Children: Catechesis and Liturgy* (Chicago: Liturgy Training Publications, 1989), 191.

11. Duggan, "Discerning Conversion," 192.

12. Duggan, 192.

The process is not to be rushed. It takes as long as it takes. The rite itself urges that "the time spent in the catechumenate should be long enough—several years if necessary—for the conversion of faith of the catechumens to become strong" (RCIA 76; also see RCIA 253). Conversion is fragile; we can expect that there may be breakdowns along the way. For instance, young children at times might show signs of resistance or disinterest, even when parents or guardians or other adults in their life continue to urge them to baptism. Teenagers, even those who seek initiation on their own, might have moments of rebellion or apathy and might need some space as they discern the Spirit's movements. What does this mean for those who walk with them in this process? Listen, be patient, and remember that all of this is at God's initiative. We can only offer our hospitality, availability, reassurance, and respect for the freedom each catechumen has to respond to God's call to faith.

Discernment

Baked into the process of conversion and the awakening of the gift of faith is discernment. It is critical that this not be overlooked for children and teens. Perhaps too often attention is not given to discernment because it is assumed that children and teens will simply move through the initiation process with their peers or according to their grade level in school. Or maybe because of busy schedules, we tell parents or guardians to pencil in certain dates on their calendars for the rites of the RCIA process before we know whether they are ready to participate in these rites.

From a practical viewpoint, this might make sense, but we might also be unintentionally setting up the expectation that the dates given *will be the dates* for their child's progression through the process. Discernment, however, is critical to the conversion process and eludes calendaring.

Who then is engaged in discernment? In the first place, the young catechumens participate in discernment. What guidance can we offer them?

One, discernment is something that happens through prayer. Hopefully, prayer has been part of the experience all along, so sorting out their own sense of readiness for each stage of the initiation process in the context of prayer will feel natural to them.

Two, what have we been doing throughout the time with the catechumens to help them listen and attend to the Spirit's promptings? In what ways has God been speaking to them? Ideally, this is a regular part of faith sharing with the catechumens.

Finally, how do we help them identify anything that might be holding them back from feeling ready for next steps? What concerns them or makes them feel unsure?

Discernment is not left to the catechumens alone but involves others. We see in the rite, for example, that before the Rite of Election,

> there should be a deliberation prior to its celebration to decide on the catechumens' suitableness. This deliberation is carried out by the priests, deacons, and catechists involved in the formation of the catechumens, and by the godparents and representatives of the local community [presumably sponsors]. (RCIA 122)[13]

For children and youth, this list would include parents or guardians. Of course, such deliberation should not exclude the young catechumens, nor should the outcome be to impose someone else's decision on them. The adults in their lives need to engage in listening to and supporting the catechumens in a prayerful sorting out.

13. Also see RCIA 43, which indicates that before the catechumens are accepted into the Order of Catechumens, there is time set aside to evaluate their motives and dispositions: "With the help of the sponsors [and in the case of children, parents or guardians], catechists, and deacons, parish priests (pastors) have the responsibility for judging the outward indications of such dispositions."

PART TWO

Chapter 5

Period of Evangelization and Precatechumenate

Preliminary Matters

Before launching into the periods of the RCIA process and exploring how we might approach the formative dimensions of the experience with children and youth, I want to clarify what the church teaches about the process of evangelization and formation.

Evangelization Every Day of the Year

The journey of faith starts with an encounter with Jesus Christ. This encounter is not limited to a particular season or time. The church teaches that this initial encounter is nurtured with the help of the Christian community, which "must always be fully prepared . . . to give help to those who are searching for Christ" (RCIA 9).

The church also teaches that the journey of faith, which takes place within the community of the faithful, is gradual and continuous (see RCIA 4). In addition, the journey from unbelief to initiation into the priesthood of Christ cannot be predetermined. The church teaches, "The duration of the catechumenate will depend on the grace of God and on various circumstances. . . . Nothing, therefore, can be settled a priori" (RCIA 76).

And the church teaches that the first stage of the journey, the period of evangelization and precatechumenate is a time "of no fixed duration or structure" (Outline for Christian Initiation of Adults). "It is a time of evangelization: faithfully and constantly the living God is proclaimed . . ." (RCIA 36).

We know from the way that Jesus constantly proclaimed the living God that there is no "start time" for evangelization. If we model our ministry on Jesus's example, we will be actively seeking and welcoming inquirers at every time of year. This means that the parish has an ongoing group for inquirers available, or, at the very least, parish staff or volunteers who are available to welcome immediately and regularly meet with those who want to explore the possibility of living the Christian life in the Catholic tradition.

Inquirers are never told, "We start RCIA in September, so please check back then," or, "The parish is quiet during the summer because many of our programs run during the school year." The thing is, the Holy Spirit is not bound by our schedules and calendar expectations, summer holidays, or organizational needs. When the Spirit opens hearts, it can feel very urgent to those who feel compelled to respond to the call to faith.

The church recognizes the uniqueness of each person's spiritual journey: "The rite of initiation is suited to a spiritual journey of adults [and children] that varies according to the many forms of God's grace, the free cooperation of the individuals, the action of the Church, and the circumstances of time and place" (RCIA 5).

An individual or a family needs to muster a good bit of courage in order to take the first step to contact a Catholic parish. This is huge! Being told to "wait" might be convenient for parish leaders but it is less than hospitable and, frankly, lags behind the movements of the Spirit. We need to be ready to welcome inquirers straightaway and begin the conversation, whether they are adults, children, or youth. When we are able to do this, the new inquirer feels affirmed; the gigantic leap they took seems less frightening and more like a step in the right direction.

To illustrate briefly, remember Michael mentioned earlier? Michael and his mother first met with an RCIA team member in March, just as the season of Lent was beginning. Michael needed to have the conversation *now;* he needed to begin to understand what was happening as he noticed rather mysterious thoughts and feelings. The last thing Michael and his mom would have needed to hear from the parish was, "We're nearing Easter and the end of the RCIA year. Can we get back to you this summer?" Thankfully, what he heard was "Welcome! It's amazing what is happening to you, and we look forward to walking with you on this faith journey. Let's get started!" For this teenager, the response communicated that what he was experiencing was good and meaningful. He and his mom were delighted—and in a way, relieved—that the parish had in place a structure that would allow Michael to bring his questions and come to know and follow Jesus Christ.

Also recall Dena and her sons, Jonah and Ian. As Dena prepared to marry Jayden and her sons prepared to welcome him into their home as their stepfather, they strongly desired to be a family with an active faith life. It was important for the parish to be able to offer them the opportunity to explore the possibility of the Catholic Church as their church home when they first called and not when a "new RCIA year" began. The immediate welcome also made an impression on Jayden, who was initially hesitant about the Catholic Church.

Another advantage of a year-round process with ongoing evangelization is that it signals that the process leading to Christian initiation is not a nine-month or academic year plan. Rather, we communicate that the work of forming Christians and their discernment about whether to be initiated into the Body of Christ is not on a timeline. The work is ongoing, and we recognize that each individual's journey will be as long as it needs to be "for the conversion and faith of the catechumens to become strong" (RCIA 76). A year-round process also takes seriously the US bishops' call for the period of the catechumenate to "extend for at least one year."[1]

1. 1986 NCCB National Statutes, 6.

Model of Catechesis and Faith Formation

The church also teaches that catechesis and faith formation are grounded in the church's liturgy and in its apostolic mission (see RCIA 75). This approach to catechesis and faith formation provides the flexibility needed for a year-round process with ongoing evangelization in that an inquirer can start anytime and be seamlessly integrated into the rhythm of the formation.

It also benefits the inquirers and catechumens, including children and youth, by getting them in the habit of preparing for Sunday and helping them to see the connections between what they encounter in the church's liturgy and everyday life. In addition, such a model of catechesis and faith formation focuses on preparing for and unpacking the experiences of the rituals that mark the steps of the catechumenate. These rituals are a critical dimension of the catechumens' experience of coming to faith and the Christian community and, therefore, are an essential source of catechesis and faith formation.

It is also vital to ground the catechesis and faith formation of catechumens in the church's apostolic mission. The RCIA is about making disciples. They join us as apprentices in furthering God's reign in the world. When we ground catechesis and faith formation in the church's liturgy and apostolic mission, those seeking initiation will come to appreciate that these dimensions of the Christian life are intertwined. As a school for Christian discipleship, the church's liturgy leads the Christian community to live as the Body of Christ in the liturgy of the world—*and* our apostolic work leads us back to the church's liturgy to be challenged, nourished, and sent once again to proclaim the Good News of Jesus Christ through our lives.

Period of Evangelization and Precatechumenate

Overview

Part II, chapter 1 on the adaptation of the rite for children does not include specific provisions on the period of evangelization and precatechumenate (commonly referred to as the period of inquiry);

however, RCIA 253 indicates that the periods of catechetical formation that lead up to and follow the steps of initiation correspond to the periods of adult initiation. Therefore, we look to part I for guidance on the precatechumenate period.

The church emphasizes that this time of evangelization "is of great importance and as a rule should not be omitted" (RCIA 36). It is intended to be a period when inquirers come to know the faith and experience an initial conversion that cause them to "feel called away from sin and drawn into the mystery of God's love" (RCIA 37). It is meant to be a time when "the genuine will to follow Christ and seek baptism may mature" (RCIA 37). During this period, the inquirers are to be given a "suitable explanation of the Gospel" and are to "receive help and attention" to enable them "to cooperate with God's grace" (RCIA 38). Further, "opportunities should be provided for them to meet families and other groups of Christians" (RCIA 38), and "prayers suited to them" should be included in this period (RCIA 40).

Questions Specific to Children and Youth

The rite itself does not provide a detailed plan for this time of evangelization and precatechumenate with children and youth. It is helpful then to ask:

- What exactly should the precatechumenate involve for children and youth who seek baptism? What do they need? And over what period of time?
- Who accompanies them? Who participates in the precatechumenate? Can we manage a mix of ages in a single group? Is it appropriate for older teenagers to meet with adult inquirers?
- What comprises a "suitable explanation" of the Gospel, and how do we help these young seekers cooperate with God's grace (RCIA 38)? How do we help them come to know and follow Jesus Christ (RCIA 37)?
- In what ways might we pray with them (RCIA 40)? When and how do we introduce them to the liturgy of the church?

- What structure do we provide for meeting families and other groups of Christians (RCIA 38), and what are the aims for these interactions? Is this the time for the apprenticeship to begin of those who want to explore living the Christian life?

A Proposed Structure

As mentioned earlier, parishes ideally are prepared to welcome new inquirers, including children, youth, and their families, immediately. For some parishes, this might mean the availability of an ongoing group of seekers, led by members of the parish staff or trained volunteers. The young seekers and those accompanying them could then simply begin the process by participating in these group sessions. For other parishes, especially those that might have very few, if any, children or youth seeking Christian initiation in a given year, staff or volunteers might need to be "on call" and ready to facilitate the precatechumenate period when the need arises.

It is desirable for the meetings with inquirers to happen regularly, for example, weekly, and at a time convenient for all. If possible, gathering on Sundays would have the advantage of more readily connecting the inquirers with other members of the community and would help them appreciate the primacy of Sunday for Christians. The length of the meetings will depend on the age of the inquirers since attention spans vary.

Also important to note is that some parishes might make their regular religious education or faith formation program with their Catholic children and youth available to those who are interested in exploring the possibility of baptism in the Catholic Church. A similar situation presents itself when there is a parish school. Children and youth who are seeking initiation might simply be placed in "religion class" with their classmates. Some cautions are needed here.

First, generally speaking, the children and youth who are seeking baptism are not in the same place on the journey of faith as their baptized peers. Presumably, the baptized children and youth of the parish or school have been regular participants in religious education and faith formation since their kindergarten days or before, and they are being raised in a household with at least one Catholic parent, guardian, or family member. At their own pace, they are already coming to know Jesus Christ and have an emerging sense of what it means to live as a Catholic Christian.

In contrast, the children and youth who are not baptized may not have had much exposure, if any, to Christian understandings and the Catholic Church. Also, recall our previous discussion about the various family circumstances presented—parents or guardians who may or may not be Christian, who may be in the RCIA process themselves, who were baptized in another Christian community and are exploring becoming Catholic. It will be important for the parents or guardians (or sponsors) to be able to participate with their child in the precatechumenate period and beyond, but this might not be feasible if their child is merged with the children and youth in the parish's standing religious education program or the school's religion classes.

Another caution is that the inquirers might get lost among their Catholic peers. Their status as a child or youth who is at the very beginning of seeking to live the Christian life could be easily overshadowed by the catechesis and related activities designed with Catholic children and youth in mind. They might be the same age or in the same school class as their Catholic counterparts, but this does not mean that they are at the same place on the faith development continuum. Faith formation is not a one-size-fit-all based on age or school grade level alone. We might also imagine for ourselves what it would feel like to be dropped into a situation where everyone around us already carries the identity as a Catholic Christian, has a certain degree of faith vocabulary, and has an imagination that is already being shaped by their participation in Catholic life. Meanwhile, we are not baptized, do not yet carry the name Christian, have little to no faith vocabulary, do not feel confident enough to ask questions let alone express our thoughts or feelings, and have an imagination that will only begin to be shaped by our contact with the Christian community. Sounds intimidating, doesn't it? And it's probably not very conducive to learning and faith development.

All of this is not to say that the Catholic peers, whether in the parish or in school, cannot be involved in the precatechumenate and catechumenate periods with the children and youth seeking initiation. In fact, as will be suggested, their participation would be desirable at various moments in the process to support the young seekers and to appreciate more deeply their own baptismal responsibilities to evangelize and welcome the inquirers.

Participants

Key questions will be, "What do we do if there is a mix of ages among the young inquirers, and what if the age range is significant?" Developmentally, seven-year-olds are different from eleven-year-olds, who are different from fifteen-year-olds—and so forth. Discernment with the inquirers and their parents or guardians (or sponsors) will be needed here. It might well be possible to have elementary and middle school children together, but we might need to think about a separate gathering with teenagers or even consider having older teens meet the adult inquirers. It will simply depend on the mix of inquirers, their ages, and particular circumstances.

Parents, guardians, or sponsors should be welcome to participate in the precatechumenate gatherings. This is one way in which the young inquirers may "receive as much help and example as possible from the parents [or guardians]" (RCIA 254.2). As discussed in chapter 3, the parents, guardians, or sponsors might also bring a mix of faith backgrounds and personal circumstances, which we need to be aware of since this can either be helpful to their child's experience or potentially derail it.

Catholic peers of the inquirers, whether from the parish or school, may also have a role here. Consider inviting a small number of them to the precatechumenate meetings. Their presence may help the young inquirers feel welcome and inspired when they see children and youth their own age interested in talking about matters of faith and engaging in parish life.

The Gatherings with Inquirers

The period of evangelization and precatechumenate is "a time, of no fixed duration or structure, for inquiry and introduction to Gospel values, an opportunity for the beginnings of faith" (Outline for Christian Initiation of Adults). The church wisely recognizes that seekers need space; in other words, they need an undetermined amount of time and a flexible structure, that is, one that is easily adaptable, to truly provide an opportunity for the first stirrings of faith. With this in mind, catechists can introduce a structure for the precatechumenate gatherings that is similar from week to week, which allows the young inquirers to become comfortable and begin to anticipate the nature of the discussion or activities. At the same time, facilitators should communicate that the stories, questions, and needs of the inquirers will shape the gatherings, regardless of what is planned. With this in mind, here is a possible model for a precatechumenate gathering with children or teens:

- *Welcome and Prayer*: Anyone who is new to the gathering is invited to introduce themselves. A simple prayer follows.[2] If Catholic peers of the children or youth are present, they might be asked to lead prayer to impress upon the young inquirers that prayer leadership is a ministry for all ages.
- *Naming Grace*: All present, including the facilitators, are invited to share an experience of grace from the past week. Of course, the groundwork must be laid here first to help the participants become attuned to the ways in which God is present and active in their lives and in the world around them. As they name their experiences, they are also telling their stories. As they tell their stories, they are telling the story of God's love and discovering being discovered. Without naming it as such, they will also develop an attentiveness to

2. We might think of the Lord's Prayer as a simple prayer to teach new inquirers; however, we also want to keep in mind that the RCIA calls for this prayer to be presented to them during the period of purification and enlightenment.

the liturgy of life. Naming their experiences and telling their stories is one way to enable them "to cooperate with God's grace" (RCIA 38). As they do so, it is important to affirm and draw upon what they name and relate their stories to Christian understandings.

- *The Word*: A liturgical-based model calls for one of the Sunday readings to be proclaimed.[3] Generally, the gospel passage would be used and for younger children, proclaimed from the Children's Lectionary. For the benefit of inquirers who are new to the precatechumenate gatherings, a brief explanation of what the gospels are and the place a gospel reading has on Sundays should be given.

After the proclamation of the text, the inquirers and others present might be asked simply to speak a word or phrase they noticed. The conversation can proceed from there, with the facilitator asking further questions about what was identified or providing insights at a level understandable to the young inquirers.

The gospel reading might be related to what was earlier named as moments of grace, to other storytelling from the group, or to something happening in the local community or beyond. This approach provides a "suitable explanation of the Gospel" (RCIA 38), introducing them to the person of Jesus Christ and to gospel values.

- *Introduction to the Church's Liturgy*: With a liturgical-based approach, it is easy to introduce various aspects of the church's liturgical life during the precatechumenate. This already happens with the use of the readings, primarily the gospel passage, for Sundays. Related to this, the manner in which a reading or gospel passage is introduced and concluded in a liturgical celebration ("A reading from . . . ; The Word of

3. If the precatechumenate gatherings happen on Sundays, it is preferable to focus on the readings for that Sunday. If the group meets other days of the week, facilitators will need to decide whether they will work with the readings assigned for the previous Sunday or anticipate the coming Sunday.

the Lord" or "A reading from the holy Gospel according to . . . ; the Gospel of the Lord") and the assembly's responses ("Thanks be to God" and "Glory to you, O Lord; Praise to you, Lord Jesus Christ") can be introduced and integrated into the gatherings so the inquirers become familiar with these brief but profound words even before they regularly participate in liturgy.

This would also be a time to introduce the young inquirers to the liturgical year. Colorful liturgical calendars appeal to their imaginations and are relatable, given that they already know the rhythm of the seasons of nature and of holidays. They might be invited to share stories of their experiences of the change of seasons and of holidays, which are easily correlated to the seasons and feasts of the church's calendar.

Intercessory prayers might also be used, providing the opportunity to talk about this type of prayer and to invite participants to add their own. Using the usual structure for these prayers and concluding with words that make clear that we pray in the name of Jesus Christ will likewise be formative for the young inquirers. And of course, the use of strong "Amens" and "Alleluias" will further prepare them to take part in the church's liturgy.

- *Questions*: There should always be space for the young inquirers to ask questions or to share what is on their minds. Of course, this adds another element of unpredictability to the gathering, but it's important for them to know they have this freedom. The Catholic peers might also be invited to ask questions to prompt conversation, if this would be helpful to the inquirers.
- *Conclusion*: The gathering may conclude with a simple prayer, perhaps in the form of intercessions. In addition, we might *send* the participants from the gathering with something to reflect upon or an action to take in the coming week that is related to the themes that surfaced during the gathering.

Meeting the Christian Community

RCIA 38 calls for opportunities to be provided for inquirers to meet families and other groups of Christians. This can be facilitated in a number of ways. As suggested, the young inquirers' Catholic peers might be invited to the precatechumenate gatherings. In addition, we might recruit Catholic peers and their families or other parishioners as prayer partners or encourage them to welcome the young inquirers and their families into their homes or invite them to participate in community activities. Notably, in doing this, we also support parishioners in their assigned role in the catechumenal process:

> During the period of evangelization and precatechumenate, the faithful should remember that for the Church and its members the supreme purpose of the apostolate is that Christ's message is made known to the world by word and deed and that his grace is communicated. *They should therefore show themselves ready to give the candidates evidence of the spirit of the Christian community and to welcome them into their homes, into personal conversation, and into community gatherings.* (RCIA 9.1; emphasis mine.)

The Apprenticeship Begins

The making of Christian disciples begins during this first period of the process. In addition to the children and youth's participation in the precatechumenate gatherings, the "genuine will to follow Christ" (RCIA 37) may be strengthened further through their involvement with apostolic activities. It is also through such activities that they will encounter Gospel values as manifested in the baptized community's outreach to the broader community. Parishioners can be supportive here by inviting the young inquirers and their families to participate alongside them in activities that appeal to these youngsters, such as a food or toy drive, a cleanup of a local park, sandwich-making for a community kitchen, or praying for a particular need in the parish or local community. Within the home, the children and youth, with the encouragement and participation of family members, can take charge of the household recycling efforts, bake cookies for a neighbor, help with preparing meals and leading prayers at the family table, or gathering coats and gloves from family members for a winter clothing drive. As Mark Searle said, faith is often grasped by trying it on,[4] and this process of trying it on can certainly begin for young inquirers during the precatechumenate period. It is evangelization wrapped in action.

Moving Toward the First Ritual Step and Next Period of the RCIA

Length of Time

There is not a defined length of time for this first period of the initiation process. Young inquirers may remain just that—inquirers—for as long as they need. This is another reason to be cautious about merging young inquirers into a standing religious education program at a parish or school. Children and teens who are exploring Christianity and the Catholic Church might not have the space they need to continue as inquirers and instead feel an unspoken pressure to move along with their Catholic peers. This would be inconsistent with the intent of the precatechumenate period and fail to honor the unique journey of the young inquirers.

It is not uncommon for parishes to add the Rite of Acceptance into the Order of Catechumens to the liturgical calendar well in advance and sometimes even before there are inquirers. In some places, especially where a school year approach to initiation is used, the First Sunday of Advent is tagged as the day to celebrate this rite, often regardless of the readiness of each inquirer. We need to resist getting ahead of the inquirers. Ideally, the Rite of Acceptance is celebrated only when we know there are inquirers who are ready to move forward in the process.

4. Mark Searle, "Conversion and Initiation into Faith Growth," in *Christian Initiation Resources Reader*, vol. 1: *Precatechumenate* (New York: William H. Sadlier, 1981), 72.

Discerning Readiness to Enter into the Order of Catechumens

In the last chapter, we discussed the importance of guiding children and youth in their discernment of readiness for each step of the catechumenate process. There is not a one-size-fits-all strategy for helping young inquirers discern the stirrings of the Spirit. Discernment is also not a separate piece, nor is it a matter of one conversation in anticipation of a rite. A helpful approach is to integrate a practice of discernment into the process from the outset, encouraging the inquirers to adopt it as a habit of heart that will not only be helpful to them during the entire catechumenate process but throughout their lives. Let's imagine how we might do this.

Prayer

As we pray with the young inquirers (and their parents or guardians and sponsors) and talk with them about prayer, we can emphasize the need to ask God to open their hearts and minds, shed light on their experiences, and help them to come to know their own hearts. This is a constant for prayer and would help them to realize that the stirrings toward prayer and faith always begin with God. This is a crucial step in developing a discerning heart and mind.

We might also teach the young inquirers the practice of the Ignatian *Examen*, which can be adapted for both young children and teens. The *Examen* is a prayerful review of the day that helps prayers discover God's presence and discern where God is leading them and how they are being invited to grow. It provides a structure that children and teens, along with their parents or guardians and sponsors, can adopt as a regular part of their day, perhaps praying the *Examen* at the same time every evening. The consistent use of this prayer form, which is, in fact, an ongoing prayer of discernment, can be invaluable to the sorting out that the journey toward Christian initiation requires. There are plentiful resources available on the *Examen*, including on ways it can be adapted for children and teens.[5]

5. See, e.g., https://www.ignatianspirituality.com and https://www.loyolapress.com.

We should further impress upon the young inquirers that discernment is also supported by the prayers of the community. To help the young inquirers absorb this, they can be encouraged to pray for one another. We might ask their Catholic peers in the parish to accompany them as prayer partners, a role that can include conversations, engagement in parish activities together, and notes of prayerful support. Further, the entire community should be regularly invited to pray for those in the precatechumenate. We can do this by adding an intention to the Sunday prayers of the faithful, weekly bulletin, or parish e-letter. We might include a commentary on the parish's webpage about the value of parishioners' prayers to those who are seeking to be members of the Christian community.

Precatechumenate Gatherings

In addition to times of prayer, there are other ways to incorporate a spirit of ongoing discernment into the precatechumenate sessions. For instance, the activity of naming grace, as suggested earlier, can help the children and youth become sensitive to the ways of God and develop a vocabulary to talk about these experiences. We read in the Bible many stories about our ancestors in faith sorting out the stirrings of the heart and responding to God's call. As we proclaim and discuss the Sunday readings, we can point out these instances and talk with the young seekers about ways they relate to these stories.

We might also periodically put before the children and youth the questions posed during the Rite of Acceptance. For example, "What do you ask of God's Church?" (RCIA 50). We can talk with the young seekers as they begin the process and throughout the precatechumenate about what they desire or need from the church, as experienced in the particular parish community. We can also tap the options for the presider's text during the first acceptance of the Gospel (RCIA 52). These texts offer rich images that we can break open with the young seekers, such as following God's light and the way of the Gospel; walking in the light of Christ and learning to trust his wisdom; committing themselves daily to his care and coming to believe in him with all their heart (from option A). They will be asked at the time of the Rite of Acceptance whether they feel ready to begin the journey of following Christ. Upon being signed with the cross of Christ, they will be instructed to "learn to know and follow him" (RCIA 55). Rather than hearing all of this for the first time at the rite, we can find moments during the precatechumenate to talk about the ways in which God is revealed, what the way of the Gospel means for them, how they can come to walk in the light of Christ, and to turn to Christ daily with a desire to believe in him. Importantly, these conversations will generate touchstones for discernment about their readiness to take the ritual steps in the process of becoming a Christian disciple.

Conversations at Home

Parents or guardians can encourage discernment through regular prayer and conversations with their children. We can do this by giving parents or guardians suggested prayers for home use that ask God to bring light and understanding and to move the young seekers to trust in Christ. They can encourage and model a daily time of reflection, such as the *Examen*.

Parents or guardians may also find it helpful to have conversation starters to assist them with talking with their children about what is happening in the process. For example: What lingers for them from the precatechumenate sessions? What do they notice when they pray? What have they learned about Jesus? What do they like about the parish community? What has changed for them? What questions do they have?

What the parents/guardians hear and what they observe in their children will be essential ingredients in the process of discerning readiness for the catechumenate and the rites of Christian initiation.

The Community's Role in Ongoing Discernment

Recall that the members of the parish are to welcome seekers into their homes, into conversation, and into community gatherings (RCIA 9.1). The young inquirers' experiences of the local church are key to discerning readiness to belong to the Christian community. In addition, community members who regularly interact with the children and youth can be helpful by praying for them, talking with them about what it means to be a disciple of Christ, and listening to the inquirers' reflections on their experiences of the process. Input from the community gives more information to the inquirers, their parents/guardians and sponsors, and catechists as they discern next steps.

Feelings and Emotions

Discernment requires attention to feelings and emotions. What do the young seekers notice about themselves, and what do we notice about them? Do they feel energized, joyful, at peace about their participation in the precatechumenate? Or do they feel a sense of dis-ease, hesitation, or confusion? Keeping a journal in which they note what comes to them in prayer and what they are feeling might be a useful way for them to know their hearts. And we should be prepared to help them speak about thoughts and emotions throughout the process. It's another critical indicator of readiness for the next stage of the journey. We rejoice with them when they feel eager and ready to move another step closer to baptism, but we also need to respect hesitancy. If they wish to remain in the precatechumenate period, let us reassure them and emphasize the community's joyful and unwavering support for them. The sorting out is specific to each inquirer and is in accordance with the Holy Spirit's timeline. None of this can be rushed; there are no shortcuts to the font.

In discerning readiness for the Rite of Acceptance in particular, we should also look to RCIA 42, which reminds us to discern whether "the beginnings of the spiritual life and the fundamentals of Christian teaching have taken root in the candidates." Is there "evidence of the first faith . . . [and] an initial conversion and intention to change their lives and to enter into a relationship with God in Christ"? Have these young inquirers begun a practice of prayer? Do daily moments of grace catch their attention? Do they and do their parents or guardians and sponsors detect a change in attitudes or behaviors? Do they have some sense of the church through experiences with the Christian community?

In a year-round catechumenal process, inquirers who feel ready to take the next step of entering into the Order of Catechumens ought to be able to participate in the Rite of Acceptance as soon as practicable. It means a parish needs to be ready to celebrate this rite as often as needed, perhaps more than once a year (see RCIA 18). This rite is not tied to a particular Sunday, liturgical season, or feast. It is a matter of celebrating the rite when it is needed and when it makes sense to do so.[6]

One question that could arise is whether children and teens should be accepted into the catechumenate at the same time as adult inquirers. One principle to keep in mind here is that there is *one catechumenate*. There is not an "adult catechumenate" and a "children's catechumenate." Yet, part II, chapter 1 on the Christian Initiation of Children Who Have Reached Catechetical Age indicates a Rite of Acceptance with a "small congregation, since the presence of a large group might make the children uncomfortable" (RCIA 260). This seems to contradict RCIA 45, which expresses a desire for "the entire Christian community or some part of it" to assemble for the Rite of Acceptance. What are we to do? The *one catechumenate* principle is critical. If we ritually separate the children, teens, and adults who are about to state their desire for baptism and ask the gathered church to support them in their faith journey, it undercuts this principle and confuses the inquirers and the assembly. As for the comfort level of the children and teens before a larger assembly, they are likely no more uncomfortable standing before the gathered church for the first time than the adults. They all experience some butterflies in their stomach, until they see the love and joy on the faces in the assembly.

In the next section, we will discuss the immediate preparation for, celebration of, and reflection on the Rite of Acceptance into the Order of Catechumens. We will then turn to the period of the catechumenate.

6. The RCIA provides only that the rite "will take place on specified days during the year (see no. 18) that are suited to local conditions" (44).

Chapter 6

First Ritual Step: Acceptance into the Order of Catechumens

Liturgical Ritual as Formative of Christian Disciples

Whether we are eight or eighty, we *need* ritual. Without it, life would overwhelm us. Without ritual, we would struggle to make sense of our lives and the world we live in; we would not discover the depth of meaning inherent in our experiences; we would miss out on a primary way of telling our stories. Without ritual, how would we learn our identity and sustain our web of relationships? In the Catholic imagination, liturgical ritual is a primary means of encountering and responding to Divine Mystery. The church's rituals also rehearse us in our role as the Body of Christ so we come to live as the Body of Christ.

Children and youth need ritual as much as adults do. They regularly participate in everyday rituals, like those performed for birthdays, sports, honors and awards, homecomings, graduations, weddings, births, and deaths of family members. These common ritual experiences shape their identity and give meaning to their lives. In other words, ritual is integral to their growth and development. For those seeking Christian initiation, their familiarity with and natural openness to ritual allows them to enter into the rituals that will mark their progress and strengthen their relationships with Christ and the church. All of this is to underscore that the rituals threaded through the catechumenal journey are essential. They are designed to affirm the conversion experience and plant within the catechumens a desire to participate in the church's liturgical life that will deepen as they live the Christian life. We cannot overstate how invaluable rituals are as a source of faith formation, contact with the community, and training for Christian apprentices.

Of course, when it comes to rituals, quality matters! Poorly celebrated rituals make for poor catechesis, do little to support conversion, limp in communicating meaning, and don't make the grade in the school of discipleship. Rituals need to be well prepared and engaging, thoughtfully performed, and celebrated with the community (RCIA 4). When this happens, the power of ritual to form and transform is undeniable.

Rite of Acceptance into the Order of Catechumens

Immediate Preparation

Once you have discerned the child or youth's readiness for the Rite of Acceptance into the Order of Catechumens, preparation for the rite is essential. We are not speaking here about a full-blown rehearsal of the ritual; rather, the preparation that is needed is one that invites the children and youth to anticipate the event in a way that will help them be present to and engaged in the rite. It is also important as we do this not to explain away the symbols. In other words, the preparation for—and the reflection on the ritual, once celebrated—is not about telling the children and youth what each symbolic gesture, movement, word, and object means but rather, listening to what they experience and providing guidance and input as needed to expand their understandings. We are forming their faith as we do so. What might this preparation look like? Here are a few suggestions:

- Focus on a few key symbols that the children and youth will encounter in the Rite of Acceptance:[1] waiting at the doors of the church to be greeted, hearing or speaking their names, being asked "What do you ask of God's Church?," being welcomed into the midst of the assembly (the gathered church), touching the book of gospels to indicate their acceptance of the Gospel,[2] being accompanied by their parents or guardians (or sponsors), being signed with the sign of the cross. With each symbol selected, help the children and youth relate it to something that is familiar and to what they have heard and experienced during the precatechumenate period.
- For instance, the young participants can likely tell stories about waiting at doors or other entrances and being welcomed—perhaps at their grandparents' or friends' homes, their school, community centers and restaurants, museums and amusement parks, and so on. What do their stories convey about the anticipation of being welcomed? What was their experience of being greeted and perhaps hearing their name? Did they act or feel differently once they passed through the entrance and were welcomed? As they share their stories, we can comment on the fact that the church has doors, too, and that they will be named and welcomed there. Invite them to pay attention to what they see and hear and feel at this moment.

1. I am assuming here that the children and youth will participate in the Rite of Acceptance with adults and am therefore looking at the rite as described in part I. If there are no adults, the ritual text provided in part II, chapter 1 may be used. I am also assuming that the rite is celebrated within the context of Sunday Mass, which, while not required, has the advantages of introducing the catechumens to a broad representation of the parish community, supporting the assembly's role in the process, and stressing the importance of Sunday in the Christian life.

2. Inviting the new catechumens to touch the book of the gospels here is an adaptation of the rite. In addition, the First Acceptance of the Gospel is in the rite as prescribed in part I; it is omitted in part II, chapter 1.

- Or show them the book of gospels and invite them to share what they have learned during the precatechumenate about the gospels. They might then be asked if they have ever touched something very special, like a family photo album, an item that holds special meaning in the family, or a gift that is brought out only on special occasions. What does it mean to be able to touch these precious things? For instance, do they feel a sense of belonging to something bigger than themselves? Do they feel part of a larger story? Encourage them to pay special attention to the book of the gospels, which will be carried in procession and, during the rite, brought to them so they may place their hands on it.
- Or, to prepare them to be signed with the sign of the cross, talk with them about their senses. What do their senses allow them to experience? Explain that they will be touched and signed with the cross of Jesus Christ on the parts of their body that enable them to experience life—their mind, ears, eyes, lips, heart, shoulders, hands, and feet. Without being told what it all means, they will have enough to help them be attentive and comfortable with being touched during the rite.

Celebration of the Rite of Acceptance into the Order of Catechumens

The Rite of Acceptance is described as being of "utmost importance." It is the first time the candidates for entrance into the catechumenate publicly "declare their intention to the Church," and the church, "carrying out its apostolic mission, accepts them as persons who intend to become its members" (RCIA 41). The movements and words of the rite communicate hospitality, joy, and love as the catechumens are embraced by the church with a "mother's love and concern" (RCIA 47). When celebrated with this in mind, the rite will capture the imaginations of the children and youth seeking to belong to the household of faith they see before them. They will feel affirmed and encouraged in their desire to know and follow Christ.

The Rite of Acceptance continues with the Liturgy of the Word, which includes intercessions for and prayer over the catechumens before they are dismissed. Assuming the rite is celebrated within Sunday Mass, the catechumens are sent to reflect upon the word of God which they shared with the assembly. This occasion should begin weekly dismissal of the catechumens from Sunday Mass during the entire period of the catechumenate. The primary focus of the dismissal reflections should be on some aspect of the Liturgy of the Word, but the conversation might also include something the catechumens noticed during the gathering rites. When the overall approach to faith formation is liturgical, the young catechumens will feel prepared for these dismissal reflections. For example, ideally, they will already be familiar with one or more of the readings for a given Sunday or other symbols encountered in the gathering rites or Liturgy of the Word.

Reflection on the Rite of Acceptance into the Order of Catechumens

The dismissal time on the Sunday when the Rite of Acceptance is celebrated can be used as a time for reflection on the rite itself. One way to facilitate the reflection is to return to the key symbols discussed in preparation for the rite. Looking back at the symbols noted earlier:

- Ask the young catechumens what feelings they had as they waited at the entrance of the church. What was their experience of hearing the presider say their name and welcome them? As they share their thoughts, the dismissal leaders can affirm their experiences and talk about how important it is for the church to welcome all who come. And we say their name to let them know that we welcome and love each of them.
- What did it mean to the catechumens to touch the book of gospels? Did they notice the same book carried in procession? The dismissal leaders can further emphasize here the special nature of the book of gospels to the community. In addition,

by touching this book, they indicated that they are learning about the Good News, the Gospel, of Jesus Christ.

- Or, if the preparation focused on the signing of the senses, invite the catechumens to tell the story of having the cross traced on their forehead and other parts of their body. As they share their stories, the dismissal leader can draw out their experiences to emphasize that each of them—their entire self—has been claimed for Christ.

Of course, it is important to be flexible and to allow for other experiences of the rite to be shared and questions to be asked. The key is to impress upon the young catechumens the value of reflecting on how the symbols of the church's liturgy speak to us individually and as a community.

Contact with the Community

As we will discuss more fully in the next section, the RCIA text makes very clear the need for catechumens to have contact with the Christian community. Celebrating the Rite of Acceptance with the Sunday Mass assembly and regularly dismissing the catechumens from Sunday Mass provide many opportunities for the catechumens to come to know the community and the community to come to know them. For example, the catechumens, along with their families, might meet parishioners at the after-Mass donuts and coffee hour. As parishioners become familiar with the young catechumens and their families, they might find ways to engage them in conversation as they arrive for Mass. Such interactions are essential not only for the catechumens and their families but also for the parishioners as they embrace their responsibilities to reach out in friendship and love to those who are seeking to live the Christian life.

PART THREE

Chapter 7

Period of the Catechumenate

Overview

As with the precatechumenate, part II, chapter 1 on the adaptation of the rite for children does not include specifics on the period of the catechumenate. We look again to part I for the approach envisioned for this stage of the process and consider what must be adapted to the spiritual progress of the children and youth, "that is, to [their] growth in faith, and to the catechetical instruction they receive" (RCIA 253).

Paragraph 75 of the rite provides the framework for the catechumenate and is absolutely essential to developing an approach to the formation of catechumens, including children and youth. The creative work of weaving comes to mind when I read this section. With the Holy Spirit at the spinning wheel, the church sets the loom and we work to weave together the threads we find in RCIA 75, which begins:

> The catechumenate is an extended period during which the candidates are given suitable pastoral formation and guidance,

> aimed at training them in the Christian life.[1] In this way, the dispositions manifested at their acceptance into the catechumenate are brought to maturity. *This is achieved in four ways.* (emphasis mine)

These four ways include catechetical, communal, liturgical, and apostolic dimensions. One cannot be omitted nor isolated from the others. We need to weave these four threads simultaneously into a holistic formation of the catechumens. In essence, throughout the process, the catechumens and the local community gradually fabricate the baptismal garments that will clothe the newly baptized for a lifetime. Keeping in mind their interwoven nature, let's explore each of these strands.

Catechetical Dimension

Paragraph 75 does not provide us with lesson plans; rather, it invites us to envision a multifaceted catechesis. This catechesis is to be "gradual and complete" and "accommodated to the liturgical year, and solidly supported by celebrations of the word" (75.1). The catechumens should become acquainted with church teachings while also being led to a sense of the mystery of salvation (75.1). What we see here is that catechesis cannot simply be equated with religious instruction; it needs to be grounded in the liturgical year, Scripture, and church teaching to lead the catechumens to an appreciation of the mystery of our salvation in Christ.

But there's more. RCIA 75.2 adds that as the catechumens become more familiar with the Christian way of life and are helped by the example and support of others, they learn to turn more readily to God in prayer, find hope in Christ, and are inspired by their developing faith in their actions, including practicing love

1. The RCIA cites Vatican Council II, Decree on the Church's Missionary Activity, *Ad Gentes*: "[T]he catechumenate . . . is not merely an exposition of dogmatic truths and norms of morality, but a period of formation in the entire Christian life, an apprenticeship of suitable duration, during which the disciples will be joined to Christ their teacher" (14).

of neighbor. Prayer and living in a way that reflects a growing faith in Christ are likewise catechetical and formative, which is strengthened when we spend time reflecting with the young catechumens on their experiences of prayer, personal and communal, and their actions in daily life.

Further, paragraph 75 anticipates that the catechumens are formed through celebrations of the word of God, including the Liturgy of the Word at Sunday Mass (75.3), and through working actively with others to spread the Gospel (75.4). In other words, the catechumens' regular encounter with the word of God proclaimed within the community and their participation with others in missionary activities contribute to the gradual and complete nature of the catechesis envisioned.

Communal Dimension

The importance of the community in the catechumenate, including children and teens, cannot be overstated. Sitting on the sidelines and thinking of the RCIA process as a parish "program" that a small group of people take care of is not an option for parishioners. The initiation of catechumens involves *everyone* in the baptized assembly; it is quite simply a baptismal responsibility. The rite itself repeatedly makes this clear, beginning with the introductory paragraphs:

> [The] community must always be fully prepared in the pursuit of its apostolic vocation to give help to those who are searching for Christ. . . . [The] entire community must help the candidates and the catechumens throughout the process of initiation. (RCIA 9)[2]

During the period of the catechumenate, in particular, the community is to help the catechumens turn to God in prayer, be an

2. Also see RCIA 4: "The initiation of catechumens is a gradual process that takes place within the community of the faithful. By joining the catechumens in reflecting on the value of the paschal mystery and by renewing their own conversion, the faithful provide an example that will help the catechumens to obey the Holy Spirit more generously."

example of people who witness to their faith, and support and assist the catechumens with practicing love of neighbor (75.2). Further, the church, as represented by the local community, is to help the catechumens through its own participation in liturgy (75.3) and mentor the catechumens in the church's apostolic and evangelical mission. We form the catechumens to be church by acting as church and engaging them in our work.

Liturgical Dimension

Importantly, the RCIA is a *liturgical order* of the Catholic Church. The rite envisions that liturgical ritual assists the catechumens on their journey, purifying and strengthening them with God's blessing (RCIA 75.3). During the period of the catechumenate, the catechumens should participate in Sunday Mass by taking part in the Liturgy of the Word and being dismissed before the Liturgy of the Eucharist to continue their reflection on the word proclaimed and preached (RCIA 75.3). The rite also provides for other liturgical experiences, namely, celebrations of the Word, minor exorcisms, blessings, and anointings of the catechumens. This ritual engagement is integral to the catechesis provided and requires both preparation for and reflection upon the rites in order for the young catechumens to discover the meanings they hold and to encounter Divine Mystery. The central nature of liturgy in the catechumenate also reminds us that the liturgy is a school for Christian disciples. We need to help the children and youth discover the liturgy's outward turn and the ways in which it forms and sends the baptized and those preparing for baptism to live as disciples in the world.

Apostolic Dimension

The fourth strand of the catechumenal framework is explained in RCIA 75.4:

> Since the Church's life is apostolic, catechumens should also learn how to work actively with others to spread the Gospel and

build up the Church by the witness of their lives and by professing their faith.

This section is inspired by the language of *Ad Gentes* 14, which describes the catechumenate as a "period of formation in the entire christian life, an apprenticeship of suitable duration, during which the disciples will be joined to Christ their teacher." The understanding of the catechumenate as an apprenticeship means forming catechumens who, once baptized, will walk around *wet*, dripping with baptismal grace and forever living out of their baptism. Of course, apprentices need mentors who walk around *wet*; they need to work alongside the baptized who are committed to proclaiming the Good News of Christ and carrying out the mission of the church.

Questions Specific to Children and Youth

How do we weave together these four dimensions of RCIA 75 when working with children and youth in the catechumenate? We will want to ask:

- How can the period of the catechumenate be structured to draw upon these threads simultaneously?
- Who is involved with the catechumens during this period? The rite envisions that the community plays a significant role. How do we educate the community about their responsibilities and create spaces for them to serve as mentors and companions to the young catechumens?
- What is the approach to catechesis to ensure that it is grounded in liturgy, Scripture, church teaching, and our evangelical and apostolic mission?
- Are the children and youth regular participants at Sunday Mass, and are they dismissed for continuing reflection on the Word proclaimed and preached? Are the other rituals we find in the period of the catechumenate celebrated with them? Mindful that there is *one* catechumenate, are the children

and youth included with the adults at Sunday Mass and for other rituals?

- Do we see the children and youth as apprentices in the Christian life? How do we engage them in the work of discipleship *now*? Who are their mentors and companions in this work?

A Proposed Structure

The first question is how to give structure to the experience of the catechumens when we need at once to draw upon the catechetical, liturgical, apostolic, and communal dimensions. In other words, what can we tell the children and youth and their parents a typical week will look like? In broad strokes, I suggest the following pieces:

- One priority is weekly participation in Sunday Mass and in the dismissal session or activity. It is vital for the young catechumens to appreciate that Catholics live out of the Sunday experience. In other words, Sunday liturgy is essential to the Catholic identity and way of life. We need to introduce the catechumens to this rhythm of Catholic life and instill in them the sense that participation in Sunday Eucharist and the work of Christian discipleship go hand in hand. An important piece of this is to help the children and youth prepare for Sunday Mass, including looking ahead at the Scripture readings assigned for the upcoming Sunday. This will enable them to be more present and listen more closely on Sunday. When the catechumens are dismissed, it will be important to spend time talking with the children and youth about what they heard in the readings and homily, even if it is simply a word or phrase that caught their attention. Or perhaps something else lingers for them from their experience—a procession, the sign of the cross, the opening song, the singing of "Alleluia," the baptismal pool, an icon or sacred art in the worship space. It's important to follow their lead and be prepared to offer catechetical input.

- The week should also include a time for extended catechesis. This could be on Sunday following the dismissal conversation. One caution here is not to omit reflection on the Liturgy of the Word or other aspects of Mass. Whether after Sunday Mass, before or after a community outreach or social activity, or a set time during the week, the extended catechesis can include preparation for the next Sunday, discussion about a particular topic and church teaching concerning that topic, or preparation for and reflection upon an experience of the church's evangelical and apostolic mission.
- The rite calls for celebrations of the Word,[3] which might be used when the extended catechesis is on a day other than Sunday. It would provide a way to anticipate the Scripture readings for the coming Sunday. Minor exorcisms[4] and blessings of catechumens[5] may also be included in the celebrations of the Word or at the end of a catechetical meeting. The frequency of these is not specified; it's really a matter of determining what would be helpful to the children and youth.
- The catechumenate also includes a rite of anointing of the catechumens, through the use of the oil of catechumens. The catechumens should be anointed at least once. This is the *minimum*. They may be anointed whenever it "seems beneficial or desirable" (RCIA 98), "several times" in fact (RCIA 100). Ordinarily, the rite of anointing would take place in a celebration of the word of God (RCIA 100); however, it can also be celebrated during the Liturgy of the Word at a Sunday Mass. Doing so would allow the Sunday Mass assembly to participate in this moving ritual. In addition, *all* catechumens who are ready, the children, teens, and adults, would be anointed.

3. The rite includes a model for a celebration of the word of God. See RCIA 85–89.

4. Several options of prayers of exorcism are included in RCIA 94.

5. Options for prayers of blessing are found in RCIA 97.

And let us not overlook the fact that these additional rituals of the catechumenate are important catechetical moments. Catechists should attend not only to preparing the young catechumens for these rituals but also unpacking their experiences.

- Participation in the parish community and in the parish's work in the broader community are also essential experiences for the young catechumens. This would include opportunities on Sundays, such as the time of gathering for Mass and social time afterward, and other times when the community gathers for prayer for parishioners of all ages to get to know the catechumens. The RCIA team should also identify the various ministry and social activities within the parish community and the extended community that would be meaningful and formative experiences for the children and youth in the catechumenate.

Participants

As mentioned with respect to the inquiry group, if the catechumenate includes children and teenagers in elementary and middle school, the catechetical team will need to discern especially with the teens whether to create a separate formation group or include them in the sessions with the adult catechumens. The catechumens' parents or guardians and sponsors should be welcomed so they too experience the catechumenal formation. This hopefully will mean that conversation, reflection, and prayer will continue at home.

The catechumens' peer companions also have a role. One, as with the inquiry group, they can be invited to participate in the faith formation sessions with the catechumens. Their presence would impress upon the young catechumens that the Catholic children and youth take seriously their own growth in faith and their responsibility to accompany and be mentors to the catechumens. Two, the peer companions can play a significant role with involving the catechumens in various activities of the parish, whether social, liturgical, or apostolic. Their participation with the catechumens in these activities would strengthen the experiences for both the peer companions and the children and youth seeking Christian initiation.

Finally, it is possible that in addition to the catechumens, there are children and youth in the RCIA process adapted for children who are baptized Christians seeking full communion with the Catholic Church. Depending on parish resources, it might make sense to include the baptized Christians in the faith formation sessions and other activities with the catechumens. What should not happen, however, is for their status as the already baptized to be overshadowed or confused with the status of the catechumens. Catechumens and candidates for full communion are not the same; the difference is *baptism*. The catechumens are seeking to be united with us in the Body of Christ; the candidates already are by virtue of baptism. Therefore, we need to avoid making it appear as though they are the same, especially with the rituals.

The Faith Formation Sessions

As previously mentioned, I am committed to the church's vision of catechesis and faith formation that is rooted in the liturgy and in apostolic mission. This approach fosters in the catechumens a desire to prepare for Sunday and helps them to see the connections between Sunday and the rest of the week. This process values preparation for and reflection on rituals as an essential ingredient in the formation of Christians. Moreover, it recognizes the catechumens' apprenticeship as disciples not as an "add-on" but as a fundamental ingredient in the catechumenal process and the Christian life.

For the catechists and others working with the young catechumens, this means the work begins with their own reflection on the readings for Sundays, the present liturgical season, and other feast days on the calendar for a given week; consideration of the apprenticeship activities the catechumens are engaged with; and attention to noteworthy happenings in the parish and broader community. From this reflection and study come the themes and topics for the particular sessions with the children and youth. Of course, the exact outline for each session depends on the catechumens themselves, that is, their unique needs as well as their age and maturity level.

A few examples may help to illustrate this approach:

- **First Sunday of Advent:** The session with the catechumens might include a brief overview of the liturgical calendar as a new church year begins. Invite the young catechumens to share their experiences of time and calendars, of anticipation and waiting, of celebrations and remembering. This sharing can easily be connected with the church's experiences and the meanings of its liturgical cycles. Or the conversation might focus specifically on the themes that surface in the gospel reading for the First Sunday of Advent, such as being alert to the ways God comes to us. Since a new church year also begins a new gospel cycle, it might be helpful to introduce the evangelist whose gospel will be proclaimed that year. During Advent, we also meet Mary and Elizabeth, Joseph and Zechariah, Anna and Simeon, and John the Baptist, who come to us wrapped in stories that draw in the young and not-so-young and help us to understand more deeply who Jesus is. Outreach activities common to the season should also be included, for example, helping with the Advent giving tree, toy and food drives, serving meals at a local shelter, baking cookies for a parish event, making Advent wreaths to sell in support of a local charity, or sending Advent notes to parishioners who need support.
- **The Christmas Season:** As with Advent, a variety of topics and themes surface in the liturgies of the Christmas season—for example, the incarnation, the Solemnity of Mary, Mother of God, Epiphany, and the Baptism of the Lord. Find ways into these topics through the stories of Scripture and the experiences the young catechumens have of the church's liturgical celebrations, including the music, preaching, and all the sights and sounds of the season. What are the catechumens discovering in these experiences? Do they see, for example, that Christmas is not a birthday party but a celebration of

God's great love for us and desire to share life with us in the person of Jesus? Having met Mary in Advent and again in the Christmas season, how are their notions about Mary taking shape? What stories do they want to tell about her? Epiphany and the Baptism of the Lord are further opportunities to reflect on who Jesus is and the many ways he is made known to us. In addition, how might the catechumens be involved with various parish and community activities, such as helping to decorate the worship space for the season, delivering the gifts collected during Advent, sending cards to children who are spending Christmas in a hospital, or visiting the residents of a local nursing home? How then can these experiences be connected with all that the church celebrates during this season?

- **Sundays in Ordinary Time:** The weeks of Ordinary Time suggest a myriad of topics for faith formation sessions with the young catechumens. For instance, for the Third Sunday in Ordinary Time (Years A and B), we might talk generally about Jesus's ministry—where he went, what he did, who he met, and who followed him. Maps and pictures might help the children and youth to imagine the places where Jesus walked and preached and entered people's homes. Who were the women and men who followed him and became his disciples? What is a disciple? What does it mean for us to follow Jesus? To be a disciple? Once again, we also need to support the catechumens in rehearsing their role as disciples—for example, helping someone in their own family or in their class at school; serving a meal at a soup kitchen for those experiencing homelessness and financial insecurity; participating in a neighborhood cleanup or doing their part in recycling efforts; and so on.

In addition to the Sundays and seasons of the church year, we need to pay attention to other feasts and solemnities, other events, such as the Week of Christian Unity, and Thanksgiving, and significant happenings in the community, whether tragedies, other concerns, or things to celebrate that call for conversation from a faith perspective.

Liturgical Experiences

The period of the catechumenate includes regular participation in Sunday Mass and dismissal of the catechumens after the homily. A key consideration for the Sunday dismissal sessions will be whether to keep the young catechumens together, even when there is a significant mix of ages. If there are teens, it might also be appropriate to have them talk with the adult catechumens. Those who know the adult catechumens can help with these decisions. The dismissal sessions should focus on the catechumens' experiences of the gathering rites and the Liturgy of the Word. What did they see, hear, touch, smell? What grabbed their attention?

There might also be occasions when the catechumens can engage in community work during the dismissal time, whether at the parish or in the broader community. For instance, maybe on a given Sunday the young catechumens help with the preparations for a parish social event or assist with sorting the food donations brought to church that day. These experiences should be tied to the call of the Gospel and to Catholic social teaching in a post-activity reflection.

As previously mentioned, in addition to participation in Sunday Mass and the rite of dismissal, the period of the catechumenate may include other celebrations of the word of God, minor exorcisms and blessings, and the rite of anointing catechumens. We need to discern what would benefit the children and youth and then be intentional about finding times to include these additional rites and to see the occasions as catechetical. In other words, we don't want to celebrate the rites simply to check them off the list but rather to celebrate them fully, draw out the meanings the catechumens find in their experiences, and relate them to what the church teaches.

The Apprenticeship: Involving the Community

Not only do we need to find ways to engage the young catechumens in the community, but we also need to educate and motivate the community to meet their obligations toward the catechumens. This is no easy task. The catechumenate in a parish can seem at times to be the purview of a select few; this might be even more the case with the catechumenate adapted for children. Yet, we need the community to step up and take an active part in forming these young Christian disciples. We need to do regular and consistent messaging about the community's integral role in the RCIA process, including in the process adapted for children.

We also need to invite the community to participate in mentoring the catechumens in the work of discipleship. We can look first to existing parish opportunities for this mentorship to take place. For example, are there opportunities for the young catechumens and their parents or guardians (or sponsors) to participate with other parishioners in various forms of prayer, such as Liturgy of the Hours, or share in experiences of visiting parishioners who are homebound? Might parishioners who visit the sick work with the young catechumens to write notes or send cards for those who are sick? The children and youth in the catechumenate might help with social activities at the parish, such as coffee and donuts, the parish picnic, festivals, simple suppers, and so on. What outreach activities are available to these young catechumens? Are there parishioners who could mentor them in getting involved with environmental justice efforts, writing letters to legislators, providing food to those in need in the local community, coordinating the Advent giving tree program, donating clothing to organizations that assist families with housing and economic insecurities—and so much more? What are the activities that the children and teens in the catechumenate can participate in with the adult catechumens? Working alongside the adults will help the young catechumens appreciate that the church is intergenerational.

We also need to be intentional about drawing a connection between these various activities with the church's liturgy to impress upon the young catechumens that the work of discipleship is fueled by participation in the liturgy and that the work of discipleship is key to ongoing faith formation. In other words, their participation with the community in the various opportunities provided through the parish is not a "one-off." These are not service projects to check off the list on the way to the sacraments of initiation. The work of discipleship *is the Christian way of life*. It is included in the work the catechumens and the community do together to weave the *habitus*, the garment the catechumens will put on at baptism and wear for the rest of their lives.

Moving Toward the Second Ritual Step and Next Period of the RCIA

Length of Time

The period of the catechumenate has no fixed duration. The rite makes this very clear. RCIA 76, for instance, reads: "The time spent in the catechumenate should be long enough—several years if necessary—for the conversion and faith of the catechumens to become strong."[6] According to the US bishops' conference, the period of the catechumenate and the period of purification and enlightenment should extend for *at least* one year.[7]

The fact that the catechumenate will take as long as necessary—at a minimum, one year—further argues against placing the young catechumens on the same catechetical track as their Catholic peers who are preparing for confirmation or Eucharist. We also need to keep this in mind if the catechumens are formed with their peers who were baptized in another Christian communion and who are seeking full communion with the Catholic Church. These groups of children and teens are not *de facto* on the same timeline simply because they are all participating in the RCIA process. We need to meet the catechumens where they are and discern their readiness for the rites of Christian initiation, and we need to meet the

6. See also RCIA 7.2.

7. 1986 NCCB National Statutes, 6.

baptized candidates for full communion where they are and help them discern their readiness for living the Christian life in the Catholic tradition. There is not a preset timeline for either group.

Discerning Readiness to Be Called to the Easter Sacraments

Once again, we need to support the young catechumens and their parents or guardians (and sponsors) in discerning readiness for the next ritual step in the process, that of the Rite of Election on the First Sunday of Lent. We do this through prayer and conversation with them. The criteria provided in the rite is that the catechumens have experienced "a conversion in mind and in action" and "developed a sufficient acquaintance with Christian teaching as well as a spirit of faith and charity" (RCIA 120). Further, they must be ready to reaffirm their intention to celebrate the sacraments of initiation (RCIA 120 and 278).

As with every step of the process, it is important to have conversations with the children and teens, their parents or guardians, and their sponsors to discern the young catechumens' readiness for the sacraments of initiation.

- Do they demonstrate a familiarity with Christian teaching and what it means to live the Christian life, appropriate for their age level, of course?
- Can they imagine themselves celebrating the rites of initiation and living as Christians in the Catholic tradition?
- Will their parents or guardians and sponsors support them in this regard?

Also, refer back in this book to part 2, chapter 5 in which we discussed "Discerning Readiness to Enter into the Order of Catechumens" (page 54). Adapt the discernment process described there to engage the catechumens and their families in a meaningful discernment process for readiness to celebrate the Rite of Election and the sacraments of initiation.

The Rite of Sending

The United States edition of the RCIA text provides for an optional parish Rite of Sending of the catechumens for election by the bishop.[8] This rite is important not only to the catechumens but also to the community. While not required to be celebrated during Mass, it makes the most sense for the Sunday Mass assembly to send the catechumens for election. After all, the catechumens have become familiar to the Sunday Mass assembly during the catechumenate, given that they were entered into the Order of Catechumens before this assembly and are dismissed from this assembly every Sunday. Being sent by this assembly serves as further affirmation and support of the catechumens—*all of them*, children, teens, and adults.

For the assembly, the rite offers "the opportunity to express its approval of the catechumens and to send them forth to the celebration of election assured of the parish's care and support" (RCIA 107). The Rite of Sending is also an ideal time for the catechumens to sign the book of the elect if it will not be signed at the Rite of Election.

As with all the ritual experiences, the catechumens should be provided with a time to reflect on their experience of the Rite of Sending for election. What was meaningful for them? Hearing their parents or guardians (or sponsors) and godparents say they are ready to be presented to the bishop? Hearing the assembly express their approval? What did it mean for them to sign the book in front of the community?

We turn now to the second ritual step—the Rite of Election.

8. See RCIA 106–17.

Chapter 8

Second Ritual Step: Election or Enrollment of Names

The Rite of Election closes the period of the catechumenate and marks the beginning of the final period, a "more intense preparation for the sacraments of initiation, during which the elect will be encouraged to follow Christ with greater generosity" (RCIA 118). The rite is celebrated on the First Sunday of Lent, unless for pastoral reasons it is celebrated on a different day (RCIA 128).

Yet, the guidance on the Rite of Election for young catechumens is less than clear. In the section of the RCIA process specific to the Christian initiation of children who have reached catechetical age, the Rite of Election is termed "optional." What is the reason for this? The 1986 translation of the Latin edition of the *Ordo* published by the International Commission on English in the Liturgy (ICEL) did not include a Rite of Election in the section on the initiation of children. Penitential rites appear in the Latin *Ordo* as the second step, rather than a Rite of Election. In November 1986, the US bishops approved the ICEL translation but added a series of adaptations, which included an "optional" Rite of Election.

Catherine Dooley notes that while labeled "optional," "the intent is that it will ordinarily be used."[1] Importantly, RCIA 279 provides that if the election of children is to take place in the same celebration with older catechumens, the rite for adults should be used (RCIA 129–137) "with appropriate adaptation of the texts."

Immediate Preparation

As with all the liturgical rites, preparation for the Rite of Election is necessary to help the children and youth be *present* to the ritual. Again, this is not a rehearsal, and it's not an explanation of the symbols they will encounter. We need to prepare the catechumens but give them space to experience the rite.

- Focus on a few key symbols to help the children and youth anticipate what they will encounter in the Rite of Election: arrival at the cathedral of the diocese;[2] gathering with the catechumens of all ages from across the diocese; the presence of the bishop (usually); the opening procession, which may include parish catechists carrying the parish's book of the elect; the proclamation and breaking open of the Word; the presentation of the catechumens and the affirmations spoken by their godparents and the assembly; the bishop's words as the catechumens are admitted as members of the elect. With each symbol selected, assist the children and youth with relating it to something that is familiar and to what they have heard and experienced during the catechumenate.
- For instance, can the young participants tell a story about going to a place that seemed really important to a variety of people—such as a sacred space (maybe they will mention their own parish church), the US Capitol or other significant buildings they may be familiar with, or a place of memorial

1. Catherine Dooley, "Catechumenate for Children: Sharing the Gift of Faith," *The Living Light* 24:4 (June 1988): 309.

2. "The rite should take place in the cathedral church, in a parish church or, if necessary, in some other suitable and fitting place" (RCIA 127).

or a national park? Ask them why the place is important (it has a history; it tells us about a group of people who share something in common). Tell them that they are going to an important place for the Rite of Election and suggest they take a good look at the building and note what grabs their attention.

- Invite them also to pay attention to the book of the elect that they signed. What are they thinking as they see it carried in the opening procession?
- The young catechumens will hear their names called. What other experiences do they have of their names being called (at home, at school, during a game, or a music or dance recital, for instance)? How does hearing their name called make them feel?
- The bishop will say, "I now declare you to be members of the elect, to be initiated into the sacred mysteries at the next Easter Vigil." They will respond, "Thanks be to God." Invite them to give special attention to these words.

Celebration of the Rite of Election

The rite explains that "[at] this second step, on the basis of the testimony of godparents and catechists and of the catechumens' reaffirmation of their intention, the Church judges their state of readiness and decides on their advancement toward the sacraments of initiation" (RCIA 119).

The election is also described as the "focal point of the Church's concern for the catechumens" (RCIA 121). The privilege to admit catechumens to election and call them to the Easter sacraments lies with the bishop as the head of the local church. After election, it is the responsibility of the "entire Church [to] accompany and lead [the catechumens] to encounter Christ" (RCIA 121). The bishop is to remind the community to give good example and along with the elect to prepare themselves for the Easter solemnities (RCIA 125).

Those who have experienced the Rite of Election would likely attest to the splendor of this rite as the catechumens of the diocese gather in one space. The catechumens see firsthand that they are part of an amazingly diverse community and rich tradition. Further, being given a new name—the elect—impresses upon them that they are entering a new period of the process, which has a different feel to it as the time for their initiation approaches.

Reflection on the Rite of Election

As with all the rituals of the catechumenate, reflection upon the experience is as important as the preparation for it. We prepared the young elect to pay attention to various symbols of the rite, so it's essential to invite them to tell the stories of their encounters with Christ through those symbols. For example:

- Return to the symbol of the cathedral (or other church). What did they notice about the space? Ask them also to talk about the people streaming into the space. Provide input about the symbolism of church buildings to the church and, in particular, why the worship space of the diocese, the local church, is special to the people they saw gathering for the Rite of Election.
- Did they see the parish's book of the elect? Did they recall signing it?
- How did it feel to hear their names called and to walk with their godparents to stand before the bishop? This is also a good opportunity to note other times their names have been and will be called during the process—the Rite of Acceptance, the Rite of Sending, the upcoming sacraments of initiation.
- They were also named as "the elect." What do they think of this new name? Did they hear the bishop declare them ready to be baptized, confirmed, and share in the Eucharist at the Easter Vigil? What are they thinking as they begin the final period of preparation for these sacraments?

PART FOUR

Chapter 9

Period of Purification and Enlightenment

Overview

The third period of the catechumenal process, which begins with the Rite of Election and coincides with Lent, is a time of "spiritual recollection in preparation for the celebration of the paschal mystery" for both the elect and the community (RCIA 138). It is intended to be a time of "more intense spiritual preparation, consisting more in interior reflection than in catechetical instruction, and is intended to purify . . . [and] enlighten the minds and hearts of the elect" (RCIA 139).

This period is further characterized by the celebration of the scrutiny rites and the presentations, which are designed to facilitate the experiences of purification and enlightenment. Finally, this period includes Holy Saturday, the day of proximate preparation for initiation with the return of the Creed and the *Ephphetha* rite (RCIA 140).

Questions Specific to Children and Youth

The language we find in the rite about this third period might feel a bit weighty when we think about children and youth. In particular:

- How do we create a time of more intense spiritual preparation aimed at purifying and enlightening the minds and hearts of children and teens?
- In what ways might children and teens engage more deeply in "interior reflection"?
- What is the role of the community during this period? How do they continue to mentor the young apprentices?
- How do we prepare the children and teens for the scrutiny rites, presentations, and Holy Saturday preparation rites?
- How do we ensure that we do not simply assume that the young elect are ready to step into the baptismal waters at the coming Easter Vigil? In other words, how do we help them to continue their discernment?

A Proposed Structure

Although the rite intimates that this third period be a time when interior reflection is emphasized, it does not indicate that we abandon the four strands of formation outlined for the period of the catechumenate. Spiritual preparation is not something that is isolated from the catechetical, liturgical, apostolic, and communal dimensions of the process. And, in fact, with this comprehensive approach, the spiritual preparation has been happening all along. With this in mind, what might the weeks of Lent look like for the young elect?

- We should continue to give priority to weekly participation in Sunday Mass and in the dismissal conversation or activity. The new pieces here will be a focus on Lenten symbols and themes, the preparation for and reflection on the scrutiny rites and the presentations, and the richness of Holy Week.
- We might approach the time of extended catechesis as more of a retreat, focusing on the Scripture readings of the Sundays of Lent, the meaning of baptism, the many resplendent symbols of Lent, and their anticipation of being initiated into the

Christian community. We should invite them to share their experiences from week to week. This will also help them to be attentive to the various liturgical rites.

- The young elect should continue to be encouraged in their prayer, both personal and communal.
- Their apprenticeship with the parish also continues. Parishes often offer various activities for the Lenten season that may and should include the elect.

Participants

Obviously, the participants in this third period include the young elect, their parents and sponsors, and godparents. As with the period of the catechumenate, peer companions have a role here. In many ways, they serve as representatives of the parish community at large and should be invited to participate in the faith formation sessions, times of prayer, and other activities during the Lenten season with the elect. They should be present at the scrutiny rites, presentations, and Holy Saturday preparation rites to pray with and support the elect. Like the adult parishioners, these peer companions have a responsibility toward the elect to "give the elect the example of their own renewal in the spirit of penance, faith, and charity" (RCIA 9.4).

The Faith Formation Sessions

The focus of these sessions for this third period will be the Sundays of Lent, the anticipation of and reflection upon the rituals for the elect, and their continuing discernment about the celebration of the sacraments of initiation.

It is possible that there are children or teens who did not feel ready to take the next step with the Rite of Election and who remain catechumens. Ideally, the faith formation work with them continues apart from the elect. If resources are limited, however, it may be necessary to keep these catechumens with the elect for faith formation sessions, times of prayer, and other activities.

In this case, we need to be sensitive to their decision to remain catechumens; we want to avoid causing them to feel as though they are "missing out" on the excitement of the Lenten rituals and the Easter Vigil. This might mean giving them their own space at times apart from the elect for their own reflection or conversation.

Also critical is *not* to include the catechumens in the scrutiny rites, presentations, and Holy Saturday preparation rites, which are for the elect only. Again, we will want to do this in a way that the catechumens do not feel excluded but rather, eager for the time when they will participate in these rituals. In the meantime, they should be welcome to be present at the rites and presentations to support the elect and share their joy.

Liturgical Experiences

Notably, the only liturgical rites outlined in the section of the RCIA process pertaining to children are "penitential rites (scrutinies)" (RCIA 291–303). This is one of the most perplexing features of this section. These penitential rites are described as "a kind of scrutiny" (RCIA 291), and it is suggested that these rites may be adapted to benefit the elect's baptized companions, that is, an occasion for baptized children to celebrate the sacrament of penance for the first time.

This attempt to combine scrutiny rites with the sacramental celebration of reconciliation is not only confusing but misplaced. One, it implies that the elect and the peer companions are around "first penance/first Eucharist" age, and as we have already discussed, the age range for children in the catechumenate is anywhere from seven to late teens. Two, the sacrament of reconciliation is for the baptized and has a different purpose than a scrutiny rite; it has no place in the initiation process. It is best to avoid this confusion and have young members of the elect celebrate the scrutinies with the adults using the ritual prescribed in part I. There is no reason not to do this, and it serves to underscore that there is *one* initiation process in the parish.

The scrutiny rites from part I, celebrated on the third, fourth, and fifth Sundays of Lent, are "meant to uncover, then heal all that is weak, defective, or sinful in the hearts of the elect" and to strengthen that which is "upright, strong, and good" (RCIA 141). These rituals are intended to "complete the conversion of the elect and deepen their resolve to hold fast to Christ and to carry out their decision to love God above all" (RCIA 141).

As with all the rituals, preparation of the young elect for the scrutiny rites is critical. By this time in the process, the elect should have at least some understanding of sin. I find James Keenan's simple yet profound definition of sin as "the failure to bother to love"[1] particularly helpful in discussing sin with the elect. We might guide the children and teens in considering times when they fail to bother to love God, themselves, family members and friends, people whose names they don't know but whom they meet in everyday experiences, the earth, and so forth. Such experiences arise out of our weakness; the scrutiny rites are intended to heal this weakness and strengthen the goodness that lies within each of us and enables us to love as Jesus does.

The presentations of this third period usually take place after the celebration of the scrutinies, with the Creed presented during the week following the first scrutiny, and the Lord's Prayer the week following the third scrutiny. These, too, are ideally celebrated with the adult elect *and* with an assembly.

Preparation for and reflection upon the presentations are, of course, key. This may be a time when the children, teens, and adults can come together either to prepare for or reflect upon the experience of receiving the Creed and the Lord's Prayer. The Creed impresses upon all the elect the wondrous deeds of God, and the Lord's Prayer communicates the reality of the "new spirit of adoption by which they will call God their Father, especially in the midst of the eucharistic assembly" (RCIA 147).

The church entrusts the Creed and the Lord's Prayer to all the elect; doing so ritually with the community gathered is especially important. In fact, the presentations might be fitting occasions for members of the community to engage in reflection with the elect on the significance of the Creed and the Lord's Prayer for the Christian

1. James Keenan, *Moral Wisdom: Lessons and Texts from the Catholic Tradition* (Lanham, MD: Rowman & Littlefield, 2004), 57.

life. This would impress upon the young elect that they are seeking to be united with an intergenerational and diverse community.

The Apprenticeship Continues

The local community's responsibility to mentor the young apprentices in living the Christian life remains. The elect should be invited to participate in Lenten activities, such as simple suppers, praying the Stations of the Cross with parishioners, days of reflection (perhaps designed for families and youth in particular), preparing Easter baskets for children in the local community, sending Easter cards to parishioners who are in ill health, and so on. Time should be built into these activities for the young elect together with the parishioners who took part to share their experiences.

Moving Toward the Sacraments of Initiation

Length of Time

The period of purification and enlightenment is specific to the six weeks of Lent; however, we need to be mindful that the freedom the elect have remains. They may at any time press pause and opt to continue in the process and seek initiation at a future time.

Discerning Readiness for the Easter Sacraments

In an ideal world, discernment for readiness to celebrate the Rite of Election is also discernment of readiness to celebrate the Easter sacraments. In the Rite of Election, the godparents testify to the readiness of the candidates to be admitted to the sacraments of Christian initiation (RCIA 131). And the bishop promises them that they will be initiated at the coming Vigil (RCIA 133).

However, it is still important to confirm and strengthen the readiness of the elect to celebrate the sacraments. It is normal for the elect to sometimes feel unsure or anxious as Easter draws near. Therefore, use the six weeks of this period to engage the elect and their parents and godparents in an ongoing spiritual reflection on their readiness for Christian initiation. Allow the scrutinies and the prayers of the community to do the Spirit's work of deepening the conversion of the elect and to ease any doubts they may have. Nevertheless, the young elect should be reassured that if they feel they are not ready, they can remain members of the church's elect and may look toward a later date for initiation.

Preparation Rites on Holy Saturday

Although the rite states "*[when] it is possible* to bring the elect together on Holy Saturday for reflection and prayer" and the preparation rites (RCIA 185; emphasis mine), we should make every effort to do this. This time together and the preparation rites themselves, only hours before they step into the waters of baptism, offer an extraordinary moment in the process that is not to be missed.

The preparation rites may be celebrated in the context of morning prayer or a Liturgy of the Word. It is a time for the elect, children, teens, and adults, to return the Creed by reciting it before an assembly of the baptized whom they will soon join. The recitation of the Creed prepares the elect for their baptismal vows and instructs them in their duty to proclaim the Gospel (RCIA 193).

The *Ephphetha* rite impresses upon the elect their need for grace in order to hear and profess the word of God (RCIA 197). In my experience, these rites are not only meaningful to the elect but also to the gathered assembly who is about to welcome the elect into the Body of Christ. Perhaps it is the intimacy of this time with the elect that deeply moves the parishioners who are there to surround them with love and prayer. Allow the powerful symbols of these rites to speak to the elect: the gathered church into which they are about to be initiated, the Creed given to them by the church and now recited to express that they too share this faith, and being touched on the ears and lips as they hear "be opened."

Chapter 10

Third Ritual Step: Celebration of the Sacraments of Initiation

Overview

We come now to the climax of the catechumenal process, and we need to read closely the introductory paragraphs to the celebration of the sacraments of initiation in both part I and part II, chapter 1 of the rite. Part I makes clear that the usual time for initiating the elect is the Easter Vigil.[1] This is echoed in part II, chapter 1, where the reason for celebrating the initiation rites at the Easter Vigil is explained, that is, "to bring out the paschal character of baptism" (RCIA 304).

At the same time, RCIA 304 indicates that the paschal character of baptism is also brought forth when the sacraments of initiation are celebrated on a Sunday. We need to keep reading here, for in the very next sentence we find further guidance: "But the

1. See RCIA 23, 26, and 207. The rites of initiation may be celebrated at a time other than the Easter Vigil or Easter Sunday when there are "unusual circumstances and pastoral needs" (RCIA 26).

provisions of no. 256 should also guide the choice of time for the celebration of the sacraments of initiation." RCIA 256 states more clearly that the Easter Vigil is the preferred time for initiation.[2] Recall also that there is *one catechumenate* in the parish, which gives further support to initiating children and youth at the Easter Vigil *with the adult members of the elect.*

RCIA 305 specifies that baptism, confirmation, and Eucharist are to be celebrated with the children and youth at the time of their Christian initiation. In other words, they are to be fully initiated at the time of the Easter Vigil. Confirmation and Eucharist are not to be delayed to enable the children or youth to celebrate these sacraments with their Catholic peers.

Participants

The children and youth to be initiated should be accompanied by their sponsor(s) or godparent(s). Of course, their parents or guardians and extended family members who will support them in the Catholic life should also be present.

On a puzzling note, part II, chapter 1 indicates that "baptized children of the catechetical group may be completing their Christian initiation in the sacraments of confirmation and the eucharist at this same celebration" (RCIA 308). This takes us back to the concerns discussed earlier about merging children and youth seeking Christian initiation with their Catholic peers who are preparing for confirmation and Eucharist. These groups are simply not the same, and having Catholic children and youth celebrate sacraments on the same occasion as initiation into the Christian community risks confusing the children, youth, and the assembly,

2. RCIA 257 seems to muddy the waters by indicating that the rites of initiation with children should not take place with the "whole parish community present, but simply represented." The Easter Vigil, of course, is a celebration of the whole parish community. As already discussed, when there are confusing or conflicting directives given in part II, chapter 1, we need to look to part I, which shows a clear preference for the Easter Vigil as the time for initiation.

and unnecessarily complicating the Christian initiation of those seeking baptism.

Immediate Preparation

The return of the Creed and the *Ephphetha* rite on Holy Saturday are the immediate ritual preparation. Ideally, these rites are followed by a time of reflection and anticipation of the Easter sacraments. As we anticipate the Vigil, it is helpful to provide a framework for the elect to help them pay attention to the many resplendent symbols they will encounter that night. This should not be a full-blown dress rehearsal for the Vigil or explanation of the symbols before they are even encountered. Rather, we want to give glimpses of the celebration, just enough to help the elect to be present and put them at ease.

Liturgical Experiences

As with all the rituals that punctuate the process, the catechists and coordinators should work closely with the parish liturgy and music teams to prepare for the Easter Vigil to ensure that the rites of Christian initiation feel fully integrated into the celebration and any special concerns related to the elect are addressed.

The aim is to prepare an engaging liturgy with "big" symbols. For example:

- a robust Easter fire and sizable paschal candle to penetrate the darkness of the night
- a slow-moving and silent candlelit procession with the elect and the assembly into the church
- an impassioned singing of the *Exsultet*
- a strong proclamation of the scriptural texts that tell us the story of salvation with sung responses woven through the storytelling
- a spirited singing of the Gloria

- a clear reading of Saint Paul's words about baptism into Christ as death and new life
- a vibrant singing of "Alleluia!" and strong proclamation of the gospel passage
- a homily that speaks to the paschal mystery into which the elect will be baptized
- a seamless movement into the liturgy of baptism with a moving rendition of the Litany of Saints to accompany the elect as they process to the place of baptism
- a lot of water to immerse the elect into the mystery of Christ and his church
- a white garment so they can "put on Christ," sturdy candles to impress upon them that they are to *be* the light of Christ in the world
- a generous amount of sacred chrism to seal them with the gift of the Holy Spirit
- a sharing of the sacred meal that invites the newly baptized and the entire assembly to say "Amen" to who they are, the Body and the Blood of Christ

Full, well-prepared, and thoughtful movements, proclamations, gestures, objects, and sacramental elements support the right and duty of those gathered to actively participate and encounter the presence of Christ in the liturgy. We should want nothing less for the elect on the day they become one with us in the Body of Christ.

Reflection on the Sacraments of Initiation

The meanings of the sacraments are realized through actively participating in the rituals. Schedule time within the octave of Easter to sit with the young neophytes, their families, sponsors, godparents, and peer companions to recall the experience of the Easter Vigil.

What lingers for them?—the crackling of the Easter fire; the massive candle blessed and lit from the fire, leading the way through the darkness; the individual candles that created a glow in the church; the deacon or cantor singing "This is the night . . . "; the many stories and images proclaimed during the Liturgy of the Word; the calling upon the communion of saints to "pray for us," as the elect processed to the place of baptism; standing before the assembly as they made their baptismal promises; being immersed in the water as they heard "I baptize you . . . "; putting on their baptismal garment; the aroma of the sacred chrism; the first taste of the Body and Blood of Christ. So much to unpack! The key is to invite the neophytes to tell their stories of the night and gently guide their reflections to name meanings.

PART FIVE

Chapter 11

Period of Postbaptismal Catechesis or Mystagogy

Overview

Part II, chapter 1 of the *Rite of Christian Initiation of Adults* states simply that a period of postbaptismal catechesis or mystagogy should be provided to assist the young neophytes and that the guidelines given for the adult neophytes should be adapted to arrange this time (RCIA 330). Significantly, this final period is described in part I as a time of growth for both the community and the neophytes, to deepen "their grasp of the paschal mystery" and make it "part of their lives through meditation on the Gospel, sharing in the eucharist, and doing the works of charity" (RCIA 244).

The community is to help the neophytes as they begin their new life as baptized persons (RCIA 244) and joyfully welcome them into the community (RCIA 246). The rite describes the period of postbaptismal catechesis as one of "great significance for both the neophytes and the rest of the faithful" (RCIA 246).

Conversion is fragile, and faith is sustained over the long haul in the context of the Christian community. The community's responsibility toward the neophytes could not be more critical, a responsibility that continues well beyond the final period of the initiation process.

Questions Specific to Children and Youth

There is no definitive lesson plan provided for postbaptismal catechesis, and some, if not many, parishes struggle with the approach to this final period with their neophytes—both children and adults. Unfortunately, neophytes sometimes think they are "done" with the process with the Easter Vigil celebration, which, of course, is not true on more than one level. They are not "done" with the process, nor are they "done" with faith formation and their apprenticeship as Christian disciples.

- How do we keep the young neophytes engaged during the period of mystagogy?
- Do we continue with faith formation sessions, and if so, what is the content?
- How do we help them deepen "their grasp of the paschal mystery" and make it part of their lives?
- What is the community's role and in what ways can they actively take part in this final period of the RCIA process?

The Faith Formation Sessions

The faith formation sessions with the young neophytes during this final period should focus on the Sundays of Easter and the mysteries celebrated at the Easter Vigil. We will want to keep them in the habit of reflecting on the experience of Sunday Mass—the gathering, the Scripture readings and homily, the celebration of Eucharist, and being sent to give glory to God through their actions in daily life. Imagine children and youth who carry this habit into adulthood.

As their engagement with the parish community continues and expands, perhaps more members of the community, especially young parishioners and families, are invited to reflect with the neophytes upon what it means to live as baptized persons. Such an activity would be mutually nourishing and support the community in carrying out its responsibilities toward the neophytes.

Liturgical Experiences

The rite urges that the main setting for this final period is the Sunday Masses of the Easter season, that is, the "Masses for neophytes" (RCIA 247). The young neophytes, perhaps attired in their baptismal garment to draw attention to their status, should participate in these Masses with their parents, sponsors and godparents, and the local community and be seated in a special place in the assembly (RCIA 248). The rite also urges that the homily and general intercessions "take into account the presence and needs of the neophytes" (RCIA 248).

This final period should be closed with a celebration held near Pentecost Sunday. For example, the parish might celebrate the Vigil of Pentecost and have all the neophytes present or ensure they are together for a Mass on Pentecost Sunday.

By now, it goes without saying that preparation for and reflection upon these liturgical experiences are essential to the neophytes' formation and hopefully will be a pattern they adopt for a lifetime.

The Apprenticeship Continues

The groundwork has been laid throughout the process for the young neophytes to be active, committed members of the parish if we have sought opportunities for them to be involved in parish life from the time of the catechumenate onward. They remain apprentices in the Christian life and should continue to be mentored by more experienced apprentices. We can support this by connecting the neophytes, their parents, and families with parishioners who are actively engaged in the ministries of interest to children and youth.

The Neophyte Year (and Beyond)

The rite suggests that on the anniversary of their baptism, the neophytes should come together "in order to give thanks to God, to share with one another their spiritual experiences, and to renew their commitment" (RCIA 250). This might mean a neophyte Mass with the bishop,[1] if it is a diocesan celebration, or with the pastor if celebrated at the parish. We should also urge the neophytes to come to the Easter Vigil, both to recall their initiation and to carry out their ministry as the assembly. We might find ways to involve them in the Vigil, such as presenting the baptismal garments to the newly baptized or lighting the candles of the assembly as they prepare to renew their baptismal promises.

Beyond the neophyte year, we hope that parishes have available to children, youth, and adults robust faith formation activities that foster regular engagement in liturgy, active participation in the parish, and a commitment to apostolic works to deepen the conversion experience that is at the core of the Christian life.

Conclusion

We began by listing the multitude of challenges and opportunities before us as we embark on an initiation process for children and youth (see pages 2–4). To meet those challenges, we have to keep in mind that this is God's work. And we need to hold fast to the framework for the process of conversion and for the apprenticeship envisioned by the church. That is an approach that is:

- catechetical
- communal
- liturgical
- and apostolic

If we can do that, we will truly form our young apprentices for mission, to live as "other Christs" in the world.

1. See RCIA 251, which calls for the bishop to meet the neophytes at least once in the year and to preside at a celebration of the Eucharist with them.